Cooking Metric Is Fun

Julia C. McCleary

Illustrations by

Jan Pyk

Photographs by

ROBERT THOMPSON & JULIA C. McCLEARY

Consultant

EVELYN D. McCORMICK, R.D.

Cooking Metric Is Fun

Harcourt Brace Jovanovich · New York and London

Printed in the United States of America

Library of Congress Cataloging in Publication Data

McCleary, Julia C.
Cooking metric is fun.

Includes index.
SUMMARY: Recipes for breakfast, lunch, supper,
salad, soup, sandwiches, vegetables, and desserts—
all using metric measurements.
1. Cookery—Juvenile literature.   2. Metric system—
Juvenile literature.   [1. Cookery.   2. Metric system]
I. Pyk, Jan, 1934-   II. Title.
TX625.5.M23   641.5   78-52849
ISBN 0-15-219961-6

First edition

B C D E

HBJ

To all cooks, young and old,
with the spirit of adventure
to make metric cooking fun

ACKNOWLEDGMENTS

I want to thank the many friends and family members who have enthusiastically contributed to this cookbook in metrics, a new field for us all.

For testing recipes and in some cases for patiently being photographed in the process, I thank these young friends and the parents who supervised: Julie, Joy, John, and Jean Beckman; Debbie Brown; Jennifer and Marilyn Cook; Scott Fairbert; Martha, Janet, Patti, and Jack Francis; Kimi and Connie Gulash; Julie Jr., John, and Julie Sr. Hornbostle; Marie and Ruth Lansbery; Billy Larson; Elizabeth, Catherine, Mary Sue, and Rachel Macklem; Hollie and Mary Mitchell; Brian and Bonnie Olson; Mary Beth, Mary Alice, Don, and Steve Ruhman; Kelly, Carol, Casey, and Jerry Sedik; Germaine, Sarah, and Marienne Skinner; Eric, John, and Diana Walker; Scott, Mike, and Mary Ann White; Lisa, Kathy, and Joyce Wong.

For recipe suggestions or advice with method, sometimes both, I thank: Ruth Bishop; Kay Blakely; Betty and Jack Brusberg; Stevie Cook; Dorothy Crozier; Clayton Daley; Betty Dopp; Lucy Eklund; Mary Louise Ely; Darlene Erbach; Monica Gallagher; Barbara and George Garratt; Lorry Garratt; Shirley Guelzow; Ann Haine; Nancy Hartman; Mabel and Clare Haugen; Sarah Hereford; Janet Hoobler; Grace Knoll; Mrs. Malcolm Jeffris; LaVaughn Kunny; Dick Lintner; Mary Ann Marburg; Eugene McCleary; Mary Mc-Cleary; Hilma Peterson; Mrs. Sam Rubnitz; Ramona Sedoric; Kamaile Wong Schultz; Eleanor Smith; Sally Stover; Margaret Sturges; Em Vigdal; Betty Walrath; Welcome and Adah Weaver; Gail West; Shirley White; Charlotte Worthington.

For their valuable help with photographs I thank: Martha Bald and Noe; Gordon and Beulah Dudek; Bill Guelzow; William Henning; Mary Skinner; Dorothy Thompson.

For their sound advice on metrics in Scandinavia, I thank Ole and Inge Stang; in Canada, Albert and Elaine Sturges.

For supplying metric measures, I thank Yale Smiley, the Foley Company; for her interest and advice, Gretchen Zeismer, Home Economics Director, the Mirro Company; for her help and advice, Dean Lois Lund, College of Human Ecology, Michigan State University.

Thanks are also due Ken Johnson, the Metal Cookware Association; the Popcorn Institute; Texas Sweet Grapefruit Association for use of the name *Great Fruit;* and the Washington Apple Growers Association.

For important input on the metric system I thank: Pat Laux, J. J. Keller Associates; Peggy Meszaros, Specialist in Home Economics, and Audrey Buffington, Specialist in Mathematics, State of Maryland; Marilyn Lillie, Fred Watson, and K. Y. Taylor, Regal-Beloit Corporation.

Julia McCleary

CONTENTS

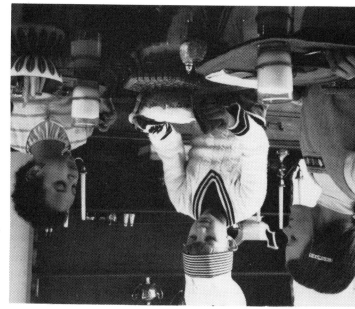

FOREWORD

An opportunity to use the metric system in preparing good meals and snacks is what *Cooking Metric Is Fun* is all about.

Julia C. McCleary is a wife and homemaker, mother of five and grandmother of three. Her home economics background provided the basics to start her family on the path to good cooking, good eating, and enjoyable mealtimes. Recipes in *Cooking Metric Is Fun* are favorites of the family and friends. They have been evaluated, tested, and standardized. As is evident in the photographs, the children who worked with the recipes and their families became caught up in the fun.

The recipes, as shown in some of the chapter headings—Breakfasts for Starters, Lunch Break and Suppertime, Salad Bar, Hearty Vegetables—reveal the many categories the young cooks explored. Of course, they enjoyed the cooking, but what makes the book so unique and appealing is having firsthand experience with the metric system, which prepares them for more metric experiences. Actually, metric recipes are easier to prepare than our current ones. All measurements are consistent within each measurement category. Educators tell us that they are also easier to memorize than recipes with the "old" system. We also know that children eat better when they have helped prepare the food.

People make food choices for many reasons: because they are hungry, because food is nutritious and helps keep them healthy, because it tastes good, and because they want to enjoy the social pleasures associated with eating. *Cooking Metric Is Fun* will help fulfill these needs.

This book provides recipes that are easily prepared with a minimum of help from an adult. Opportunities must be made available if a child is to have cooking experience. Successful independent food preparation can stimulate growth and can give the young chef experience in planning well-balanced meals. Some of the recipes are quickly and easily prepared. Others require more preparation and should be saved for less busy times or for those who have some knowledge of cooking.

Throughout the book Mrs. McCleary has woven in important facts about nutritious meals, attractiveness of the food, harmonizing of colors and shapes, variances in texture, and appropriate flavor combinations.

Having worked closely with the author during its development, I can highly commend this book. The recipes have been tested and enjoyed; metric measurement as part of the learning process has been emphasized. Everyone who shared in the planning has begun to enjoy metric cooking.

Cooking Metric Is Fun and nutritious eating go together.

Evelyn D. McCormick, R.D.
Nutritionist-Manager
Professional Communications
Gerber Products Company
December 1978

LET'S TRY METRIC COOKING

Cooking in metric is easy, and it's fun. All you need is a set of metric measures and a recipe.

Almost everything in this book is measured in volume, just as your familiar cups and teaspoons measure volume. But our volume measure is the world standard liter, which is just a little more than a quart. Every country in the world uses this standard except Borneo, Brunei, Liberia, and South Yemen—and the United States. Perhaps by the time you read this, they will have changed, too. The United States has been gradually changing to metric since 1975, when Congress made a metric conversion law.

In the old days it was never very satisfactory to pass along recipes that used a handful of this or a cupful of that because there was no real standard. How big was the hand that measured the flour? Was it heaping? Was milk measured in your small teacup or my large coffee cup? Even ancient people adopted standards, but many were the arguments started in the shops as well as the kitchen over lack of standards. In cooking, when liquid was measured by pouring up to a line marked on a jar or a bowl, it was important that the jars or bowls were always the same size. But they seldom were. This made good cooking very difficult. At last in 1791, after much study, the French National Assembly adopted the metric system as standard.

The metric system is based on multiples or divisions of ten. You will have no trouble cooking with divisions of a liter because the divisions are

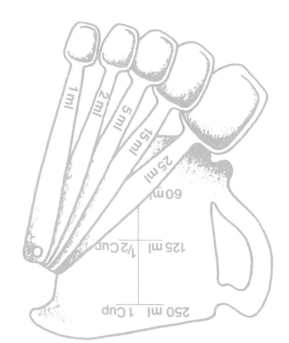

Almost the same as your familiar cups and tea-spoons. Think of a liter as a little more than a quart. Your familiar measuring cup is one-fourth of a quart, so your metric measuring cup is one-fourth of a liter: 250 milliliters (mL).

Just as we know the number of teaspoons in a cup and a quart, we know there are 1,000 milliliters in a liter. It is very simple. One tea-spoon is about 5 milliliters, one tablespoon about 15 milliliters. All you need to cook everything in this book are sets of metric measures. They will give you the amounts exactly—there's no con-version.

Equipment You Will Need

You will need metric measures in 250 mL, 125 mL, and 50 mL sizes; and measuring spoons in 25 mL, 15 mL, 5 mL, 2 mL, and 1 mL sizes. They can be found in many housewares departments and cooking equipment stores. Everything else is probably right in your kitchen. Any nonbreakable glass, metal, or plastic dish makes a good mixing bowl. You can use the same pans for metric cooking that you or your parents have been using all along, but you will notice that each recipe measured in metric makes just a little more than similar recipes based on traditional measurements. New metric pans are of course in centimeters and liters.

Where weights of meat are given, we use both grams and pounds to make shopping easier until the changeover is complete.

Before You Begin

Decide what you want to cook and then ask permission. Check the cupboard and refrigerator, too. You wouldn't want to start Oven-Scrambled Eggs and then find out there are only five eggs in the fridge! Or worse, you wouldn't want to use the eggs and then discover that your mother had planned to use them in a cake or a soufflé. So ask permission of whoever does the cooking at your house.

11

When you are ready to start, wash your hands, read the recipe all the way through, and assemble everything you will need. If you do not understand any of the cooking terms used, look at the definitions on page 21. Also look at the list of pan sizes on page 20 if you are not sure just what size pan to use.

When a recipe calls for lettuce or for any fresh vegetable or fruit, be sure to wash it thoroughly in cold water and dry before using. Carrots and potatoes should always be peeled before washing unless the recipe says do not peel. When using green peppers, wash, cut in half, and remove the stem, seeds, and the white pith before chopping or slicing. Onions of course must be peeled before using.

You will see that throughout the book the easy recipes are marked with one asterisk (*) next to the title, moderately hard are indicated by two (**), and recipes for more experienced cooks are marked with three (***). At the end of many recipes, "go-with" foods are listed so that you can plan complete meals. There are also some single-pot meals and some oven-combination meals.

Both Celsius and Fahrenheit temperatures are given so you will have no problem with your conventional oven temperatures. Metric cooking is really fun. Give it a try!

SOME SAFETY RULES YOU MUST FOLLOW

Cooking can be fun, but you have to follow the rules, just as you would in any game or sport. In cooking, in addition to following the rules of the recipe, there are safety rules you must follow.

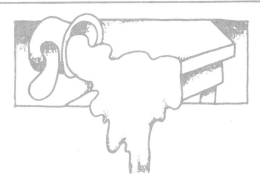

First, if you have long hair, tie it back to keep it from getting in the food—or near a flame. Find yourself an apron or an old shirt and roll the sleeves up high. Sleeves have a way of catching on pan or pot handles and upsetting them. You could burn yourself as well as spoil the dish you are working on. A good rule is always to turn pot handles away from the edge of the stove so that they cannot be accidentally tipped. When stirring anything in a pot, always hold the handle with a potholder to steady the pot. If you remove a cover from a pot, tilt it so that the steam escapes from the back of the pot and doesn't touch your hands or face.

If you have never cooked before or do not know how to manage kitchen equipment by yourself, ask an adult to stay and help you. Get an adult to show you how to use the stove, and especially how to cook with fat, which tends to spatter when hot and can easily burn you. If you can't manage sharp knives very well, get adult help when slicing or chopping or cutting up things. Always cut away from you and use a cutting board.

Never turn electric appliances on or off with wet hands. And always be especially cautious with beaters and rotary blades.

When you remove dishes from the oven or pots from the stove, remember to first turn off the burner or oven, to use potholders, and to put the dishes or pots on heat-proof mats (never directly on countertops).

Low or medium heat is usually preferred to high heat. Foods cooked over medium heat are

less likely to burn or boil over. If your stove is an electric one, remember that the burner stays hot even after the red glow disappears.

If you are cooking with an enameled-lined or teflon-coated casserole or pan, be sure to mix or stir with a wooden spoon since a metal one could scratch the surface.

Safety really does come first, and every cook must follow the rules.

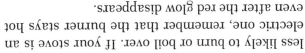

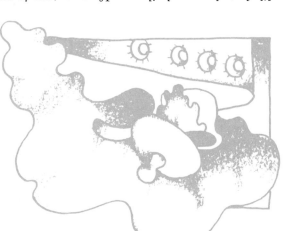

What Every Cook Should Know

If the food you cook looks attractive, then everyone will want to eat it. Right? So planning a pretty plate is part of being a good cook.

That means choosing "go-together" foods that complement each other. You wouldn't serve spaghetti, cauliflower, and baked fish together on a white plate. It wouldn't look good, even garnished with parsley. And you probably wouldn't think it tasted very good, either. That plate would have the blahs.

But try combining meatballs, green beans, and a baked potato with a pat of butter on it, and you've got something worth sitting down to the

table to see as well as to eat. Make a fruit salad, too, and you have a dandy-looking meal. It would also be nutritionally balanced.

Try to think of different combinations of food that have interesting colors, like carrots and peas. Combine them with a chicken drumstick and some curly spaghetti or rice with parsley. Give your eye something to "eat" as well—the food will always taste better.

You wouldn't plan to serve sweet potatoes with squash. They are too much alike. Combine soft things with crunchy things, and round shapes like meatballs with leafy things like spinach. Then add a sprig of parsley or a radish rose.

You will notice that all through this book we have suggested you do little things such as slice a radish thin and add it to the potato salad. That's for looks. Just a little thing like the red on a radish slice can make you enjoy potato salad more.

Other foods you can use for garnish to make a plate look more attractive are cucumber slices, sliced olives, a piece of pimento, pickle slices, onion rings, croutons, or bacon bits.

Try a bit of eye appeal when you serve to be an extra-special cook.

THE OVEN PAGE

The oven is a cook's best friend. Baking, or oven cookery, is great because the food cooks without you. With a timer or an eye on the clock to remind you, you can read or play while whole dinners are cooking in the oven. It will save precious energy if you find recipes that can bake together. Try baking potatoes and meat loaf at the same time, or chicken and Impossible Pie.

You will find many other good "oven buddy" recipes in this book.

Don't worry about converting Fahrenheit temperatures to Celsius. Just use the Fahrenheit temperatures until your oven is converted. Of course, if your oven is already converted, use just the Celsius and forget the others.

Oven Temperatures

Celsius		Fahrenheit
90	is almost the same as	200
110	" " " " "	225
120	" " " " "	250
150	" " " " "	300
160	" " " " "	325
175	" " " " "	350
190	" " " " "	375
200	" " " " "	400
220	" " " " "	425
230	" " " " "	450
250	" " " " "	475
260	" " " " "	500
290	" " " " "	550

These figures have been rounded off to be practical.

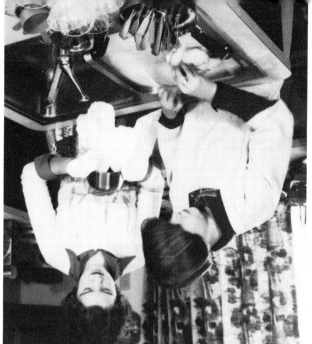

CLEANUP

Cleaning up is part of cooking. To make it easier, rinse as you cook and as you clear. You don't have to use a lot of water to rinse. Have a cooking pan ready with hot soapy water and pop the silverware from the table into it right away. Scrape and stack the dishes. Put similar things together and rinse them all at once.

Try to get a helper when it's time to wash. In a pan of hot soapy water, wash the glassware first, then the silver. Plates and cups next, then the pots and pans. Change the water if it loses its foam.

Rinse in a big pan of the hottest water you can stand. Put the washed and rinsed dishes in a dish drainer or turn them upside down on a clean towel spread on a cookie sheet. They will partially dry as they cool. All you need is a quick polish and you can put them away. Use rubber gloves if the water is too hot.

If you have a helper, one washes and one dries and puts away. It's fun. The best cooks always wipe the counters and the stove, and clean the sink.

METRIC EQUIVALENTS

Many traditional recipes can be converted to metric with a little experimenting. A few recipes don't easily convert, but using the following approximate equivalents should give you satisfactory results for many recipes in traditional cookbooks.

1 quart	1000 mL, or 1 liter
1 cup	250 mL
½ cup	125 mL
⅓ cup	80 mL
¼ cup	60 mL
1 Tablespoon	15 mL
1 teaspoon	5 mL
½ teaspoon	2 mL
¼ teaspoon	1 mL

milliliters	mL
liters	L
centimeters	cm
grams	g
kilograms	kg
degrees Celsius	°C

BOWL AND PAN SIZES

	Approximate Metric Measure	Approximate Traditional Measure
Bowls for Mixing		
Small, cup size	250 mL	1 cup
Medium	1–2 L	1–2 qt.
Large	3–4 L and up	3–4 qt.
Frying Pans		
Small	15–18 cm	6–7 in.
Medium	20–23 cm	8–9 in.
Large	25–30 cm	10–12 in.
Saucepans		
Small	250 mL	1 cup
Medium	1–2 L	1–2 qt.
Large	2–3 L and up	2–3 qt. and up
Casseroles		
Small	1 L	1 qt.
Medium	1.5–2 L	1.5–2 qt.
Large	2–3 L and up	2–3 qt. and up

SOME COOKING TERMS

BAKE: Cook in the oven.

BEAT: Stir vigorously with a spoon or electric mixer.

BLEND: Mix thoroughly with a spoon or electric mixer.

BOIL: Heat on the stove until mixture bubbles on top, 100 degrees C (212 F). This is the boiling point.

BROIL: Cook by direct heat usually from above in a stove, generally on a rack.

BROWN: Fry on both sides in a little fat until food looks brown.

CHOP: Reduce to small pieces with a knife or chopper.

CREAM: Blend thoroughly, with a spoon or electric mixer, as with sugar and shortening.

CROUTONS: Small toasted and flavored bread cubes sometimes used as a garnish with soups and salads.

CUT IN: Mix, using two knives scissor-fashion.

DASH: A small quantity, less than 1 mL. Usually refers to salt, pepper, or other spice.

DEEP-FRY: Cook by frying in a large amount of fat. Do this only with adult supervision.

DICE: Cut into very small cubes.

DOT: Scatter small bits, such as butter, over the surface of food.

FOLD IN: Mix one ingredient gently with another by turning one part over another while turning the bowl.

FRY: Cook over direct heat in butter or oil in a heavy shallow pan.

GRATE: Reduce to small particles by rubbing against a grater.

GREASE: Coat the bottom and sides of a baking dish with some kind of fat or shortening.

GRILL: Cook over direct heat, sometimes outdoors.

KNEAD: Work dough by pressing, pulling, folding, and turning.

MIX: Combine ingredients while stirring.

PARE: Cut off the outer skin with a knife.

PINCH: A small quantity, less than 1 mL.

POACH: Cook gently in hot liquid that is kept just below the boiling point.

ROAST: Cook, usually uncovered, in a hot oven.

SAUTÉ: Cook in small amount of fat or oil on top of the stove.

SCALD: Heat to a temperature just short of the boiling point (bubbles will appear at the sides of the pot).

SHORTENING: Any fat or oil used in cooking.

SHRED: Cut or tear into very narrow strips.

SIFT: Pass flour or other ingredients through a sifter or sieve.

SIMMER: Cook by keeping heat just below boiling point, 85–95 degrees C (185–210F).

STIR: Mix ingredients with a spoon in a bowl or pan.

TOAST: Brown in oven or toaster.

WHIP: Beat vigorously with an electric mixer or a hand beater.

RECIPES IN THIS BOOK

How to Use This Book

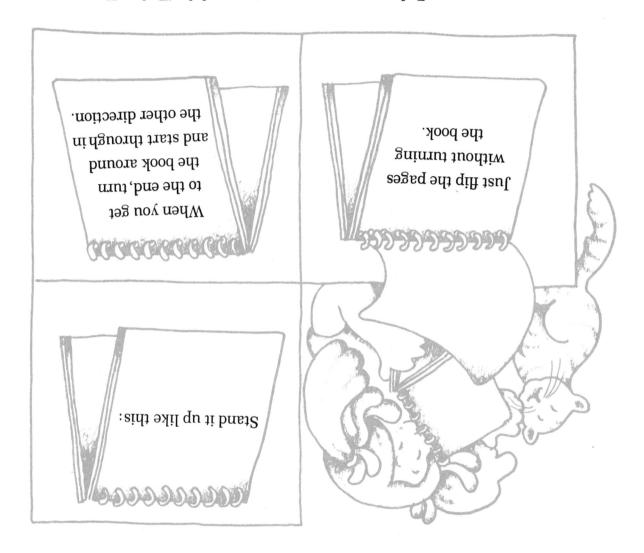

Stand it up like this:

Just flip the pages without turning the book.

When you get to the end, turn the book around and start through in the other direction.

REMEMBER: Before you start any recipe, read the "Before You Begin" section on pp. 11–12 and the safety rules on pp. 13–14.

Breakfasts
for
Starters

EVER-READY BRAN MUFFINS**

Equipment you will need:
Large mixing bowl
Medium-sized bowl
Muffin pans, either nonstick or with paper liners
Mixing spoon
Sifter

Ingredients:

Boiling water	250 mL
100% bran cereal	250 mL
Margarine	125 mL
Sugar	300 mL
Eggs	2
Flour, sifted	625 mL
Baking soda	12 mL
Salt	2 mL
Buttermilk	500 mL
All-Bran cereal (shreds, different from above)	500 mL

This recipe makes a lot of muffins. Depending on the size of your muffin pans, it makes either 3½ dozen or 7 dozen. But you don't have to eat them all at once. The batter keeps up to three weeks in the refrigerator. Bake a dozen one day and just save the batter in a covered jar. When you're hungry for more muffins, there it is, all mixed. One day add nuts; the next time add raisins or chopped dates. You're going to like these muffins.

First, combine the boiling water and the 100% bran cereal in the medium-sized bowl and set aside.

In the large bowl, cream the margarine and sugar together until well mixed. Add the eggs and stir well. Put the flour, baking soda, and salt together in the sifter and add alternately with the buttermilk to the shortening-sugar-egg mixture. When well mixed, add the 100% bran cereal and the All-Bran.

If you want to bake just a dozen, take out a little less than one-third of the mixture and add 125 mL chopped nuts or raisins or dates for each dozen. Fill the muffin cups half full.

Bake in a preheated oven 200 degrees C (400 F) for 15–20 minutes.

GREAT FRUIT ALASKA**

Equipment you will need:
Sharp knife or grapefruit tool
Flat baking pan with edges
Medium-sized bowl for beating egg whites
Egg beater

Ingredients:

Grapefruit	2
Dash of salt	
Egg whites	2
Light brown sugar, packed	30 mL
Coconut, shredded	45 mL

Cut the grapefruits in half, holding the stem end in one hand. Pick out any seeds. Cut down between the sections on each side of the membrane so each section will come out easily. Then cut around the outside. Sprinkle each with a little salt.

Preheat oven to 160 degrees C (325 F). Separate the egg whites from the egg yolks. (Directions are on page 30.) In a medium-sized

bowl beat the egg whites until they form soft peaks. Gradually add the sugar while continuing to beat the egg whites until stiff peaks are formed. Fold in about two-thirds of the coconut and save the rest to sprinkle on top.

Spread the egg whites on top of each grapefruit half, making sure the mixture goes to the edges. Sprinkle the remaining coconut on top. Bake for 20 minutes or until the meringues are browned. Serve warm. Serves 4 people.

There are other great ways to serve this vitamin C-loaded fruit, especially the big juicy pink ones. Here are three ways:

Serve them in sections. Each section wears a jacket. To get the sections out whole, peel off the outside skin with your fingers and then break the fruit open carefully into two halves. With a sharp knife, cut the membrane from the outside of the first section and peel it back carefully away from you. Keep your fingers away from the blade. Slide your knife between the partially peeled section and the next membrane. Then just tip it out with your knife. There, you already have one whole section. Now go on and take the jackets off the rest, one at a time.

You can also squeeze the grapefruits and serve the juice. Like its cousin the orange, the grapefruit makes delicious juice.

Serve in the half-shell. Cut in half as for Great Fruit Alaska and cut around each section for easy eating. Put a cherry in the center for fun. This also makes an excellent dessert for lunch or dinner.

BANANA BREAD**

Equipment you will need:
Large mixing bowl
Loaf pan for bread, 13 x 24 cm (5½ x 9½ in.)
Mixing spoon
Sifter
Smaller bowl to mash bananas

Ingredients:

Ripe bananas, mashed	250 mL (about 2 large)
Soft shortening	30 mL
Sugar	250 mL
Egg	1 large
Milk	175 mL
Flour	750 mL
Baking powder	20 mL
Salt	5 mL
Walnuts or pecans, chopped	250 mL

There's an old song that goes, "Never keep bananas in the refrigerator." But if you don't, what can you do when they get too ripe? Make Banana Bread, of course. It takes a bit of muscle to mix.

First, mash the ripe bananas. Slice them and mush them with a big spoon or a masher until they are smooth. It takes about two big bananas to fill a 250-mL measure.

Cream the shortening and sugar together and beat in the egg. Add the ripe bananas and milk and mix well.

Put the flour, baking powder, and salt in the sifter and sift into the banana mixture. Mix together and then stir in the chopped nuts. Walnuts are best, but if you have pecans in the cupboard, use them.

Pour everything into a well-greased loaf pan and let stand 20 minutes. Bake in a preheated oven at 175 degrees C (350 F) one hour and 15 minutes or until a toothpick inserted in the center comes out clean.

Don't worry if the top cracks during baking. It's supposed to. Banana Bread is a super snack. It can also make a super school lunch with carrot sticks and celery. Make a banana bread sandwich with cream cheese. Good for you, too.

HOT FRUIT COMPOTE*

Equipment you will need:
Rectangular baking dish, 17 x 26 cm
Large spoon

Ingredients:

Pear halves, drained	1 can, 454 g (16 oz.)
Peach halves, drained	1 can, 454 g (16 oz.)
Several maraschino cherries	
Brown sugar	50 mL
Cinnamon	2 mL
Butter or margarine	15 mL

Let's hear it for a Mother's Day breakfast cooked by the kids! Serve this Hot Fruit Compote and bake it along with the Oven-Scrambled Eggs (page 33). You may substitute any combination of canned fruit—apricots and pineapple, perhaps.

Arrange the fruit in the baking dish, decorating with the maraschino cherries. Sprinkle with sugar and cinnamon and dot with butter. Bake at 175 degrees C (350 F) for 25 minutes. Makes 4–6 servings.

If you are making a special breakfast, you can warm rolls or coffee cake right in the same oven in an aluminum pan or on a cookie sheet. Serve with a glass of milk and with hot tea or coffee for the grownups.

You could try this dish as a dessert, too.

Scald the milk in the large mixing pan. Add the margarine. Add the salt and sugar (for the Whole Wheat Bread the honey and molasses instead of sugar) and stir until dissolved. Set it aside while you measure and sift the flour into the medium-sized bowl. (Sift only the white flour when making the Whole Wheat Bread.) Add the dry yeast to the flour and mix it very well.

When the milk mixture is lukewarm, add the water to it and begin stirring in the flour and yeast mixture. When the dough forms a big lump and cleans the sides of the mixing pan, turn it out on a lightly floured board and cover with a kitchen towel for 10 minutes. Wash and dry the big mixing pan and grease the inside of it. Set it aside.

Begin kneading the bread with clean floured hands. Pull the dough into a flat circle. Fold one side over on itself and push down firmly but gently. Move dough a quarter turn, fold over, push down, and repeat. This is kneading. Keep on for about 10 minutes, until the dough is smooth and elastic. Turn into the big greased pan, wipe the inside of the pan with the dough, and turn the greased side of the dough up. Cover with a damp towel and set aside in a warm place to rise. When it has doubled in bulk, push down and allow it to rise again. This will take several hours.

Divide the dough into two loaves. Flatten and roll out with a rolling pin into a circle, fold in the sides, and roll up. Fit into the greased bread tins. Grease the tops, cover with a damp cloth, and allow to rise again. It should rise above the tops of the tins.

Preheat the oven to 220 degrees C (425 F) for the White Bread and bake 20–25 minutes.

For the Whole Wheat Bread preheat the oven to 190 degrees C (375 F) and bake about 50 minutes.

Cool the loaves on a rack on their sides. Each recipe makes two loaves.

The Whole Wheat Bread will not rise quite as high as the White Bread.

94

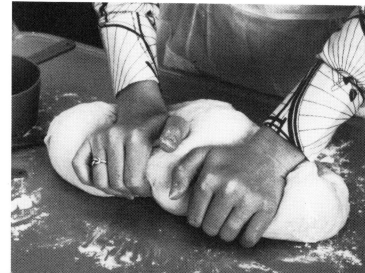

OVERNIGHT OATMEAL*

Equipment you will need:
Double boiler, 1–1½ L, glass or stainless steel
Large wooden stirring spoon

Ingredients:	
Milk or water	500 mL
Salt	1 mL
Oatmeal, regular	250 mL
Raisins, seedless	50 mL

Some days you would rather sleep late than take the time to make a good breakfast in the morning. That's the time to cook breakfast the night before. Overnight oatmeal is even better warmed up. Be sure to use the regular oatmeal because the quick-cooking kind doesn't work in this recipe.

Use just the top of the double boiler and bring the water or milk, salt, and oatmeal to a boil in it, stirring constantly. Don't let it boil over—it's hard to clean up. Add the raisins and turn off the burner.

Fill the bottom of the double boiler with about 5 cm water. Bring it to a boil with the top part in place. Turn the heat low, and cook the oatmeal, covered, over the hot water for about 20 minutes.

Turn off the burner and go to bed.

In the morning, before getting dressed, add more water to the bottom of the double boiler if needed. Turn on the burner low and get ready for school. Breakfast will be ready when you are.

With fruit or juice, a slice of buttered toast, and a glass of milk, this is a first-class breakfast. Serves 4.

TWO BREAD RECIPES***

Equipment you will need:
Large mixing pan, at least 4 L, which will go on
    the burner, or Dutch oven
Mixing bowl, 2 L or more
Old-fashioned bread board or clean kitchen top
Sifter
Rolling pin
Big stirring spoon
2 bread tins

White Bread

Ingredients:

Milk, pasteurized skimmed or reconstituted dry	500 mL
Margarine	30 mL
Salt	15 mL
Sugar	45 mL
Unbleached white flour	1750 mL (measure 250 mL seven times)
Dry yeast	2 envelopes
Lukewarm water	125 mL

The equipment you will need and the method of mixing will be the same for White Bread and Whole Wheat Bread.

Whole Wheat Health Bread

Ingredients:

Milk, pasteurized skimmed or reconstituted dry	500 mL
Margarine	125 mL
Salt	15 mL
Honey and molasses mixed half and half	125 mL
Dry yeast	2 envelopes
Unbleached white flour	500 mL
Rye flour	125 mL
Wheat germ	125 mL
Stone ground whole wheat flour	1 L
Lukewarm water	125 mL

Many people love to bake bread, but it takes a special kind of cook to make good bread. You must be sensitive to what the bread is doing and learn to know when to knead it, when to stop, and how warm it should be. Don't be discouraged if it is not quite right the first time. Try again. Follow the directions closely.

Bread dough likes a warm room about 27 degrees C (80 F) or a little warmer. You might want to try White Bread first because it's a little easier.

THE INTERNATIONAL EGG*

Oeuf   Ei   Uovo   Huevo   Agg   Ey

Soft-boiled: Take an egg out of the refrigerator and put it in a small pan of cold water to cover. Bring to a boil, turn down the heat, and simmer 3–4 minutes, using a timer or clock. Lift out with a slotted spoon and rinse under cool water. Break or cut in two with a sharp knife and scoop the insides out. You may need some help with this. Eat on toast or from an egg cup.

Hard-boiled: Simmer the egg for 15–20 minutes. Cool in cold water and peel off the shell.

Fried Egg Sunny Side Up: Melt about 5 mL butter or margarine in a frying pan. Open the egg onto a saucer without breaking the yolk. Slide the egg gently into the pan and cook until set. Cover the pan for one minute while it cooks over a low heat. Lift out with a spatula when the egg is done to your taste.

Poached Egg: Bring a small saucepan or frying pan of salted water to a boil. Break an egg onto a saucer and carefully slide it into the boiling water without breaking the yolk. Lower the heat. In two or three minutes, lift it out with a slotted spoon. Serve on buttered toast.

Scrambled Egg: Break an egg into a small bowl. Add 5 mL milk for each egg and stir well. Melt 5 mL butter or margarine in a small frying pan over low heat. Pour in the egg mixture and heat slowly, turning and mixing until set.

Learn to Bake Bread

To Separate an Egg: Have two bowls ready. Tap the egg firmly on the side of one bowl and keep the yolk in half of the shell while the white falls into the bowl. Transfer the yolk to the other half of the shell as the white separates from it so you have only the yolk left in the shell. Carefully place the yolk in the second bowl.

FRIENDLY SLOPPY JOES**

Equipment you will need:
Large frying pan
Paring knife
Medium-sized casserole with lid

Ingredients:

Ground beef	500 mL (560 g, about 1¼ lbs.)
Onion, chopped	1 large
Green pepper, chopped	1 large
Sugar	30 mL
Prepared mustard	30 mL
Vinegar	30 mL
Salt	5 mL
Catsup	200 mL
Hamburger buns	8

Sloppy Joes make a great Sunday night supper with a tossed salad and plenty of milk to drink. And for the gang after a game they can't be beat.

Early in the day, brown the ground beef in the frying pan. A little salt in the pan will help keep the meat from sticking. If the beef seems greasy, carefully skim off some of the fat into an empty metal can. Add the rest of the ingredients. If you can't get all the catsup out of the bottle, add a little warm water and swish it around. Then add that, too. Stir and heat until the mixture bubbles. Transfer to the casserole, cool for a few minutes, cover, and refrigerate.

Ask your mother or an older sister to remove the casserole from the refrigerator about an hour and a quarter before you expect to arrive with your friends and then a little later to put it in the oven for you. It will need to bake about 45 minutes at 175 degrees C (350 F). Serve in buns. Makes 8 Sloppy Joes.

WESTERN OMELET**

Equipment you will need:
Divided omelet pan *or* medium-sized frying pan
Plastic spatula
Medium-sized bowl
Wire whisk or egg beater

Ingredients:

Eggs	4
Milk	15 mL for each egg
Salt	1 mL
Pinch of pepper	
Butter or margarine	15 mL
Green pepper, chopped	25 mL
Onion, chopped	5 mL
Ham, chopped (optional)	25 mL

Break the eggs into a bowl. Add milk, salt, and pepper and beat vigorously until well mixed. Melt butter in the omelet pan (use both sides) or the frying pan. Pour half the egg mixture into each side of the omelet pan. If you are using a frying pan, pour it all into the pan. Turn the heat to medium and watch carefully. When the bottom begins to cook, hold the handle of the pan with a potholder or mitt and with your other hand carefully use the spatula to lift part of the sides of the omelet where it is stiff, allowing some of the uncooked egg mixture to run underneath. Do this all around the sides. Keep the heat on low to medium and continue until most of the egg is set. Sprinkle the green pepper and onion on top. Continue cooking until the omelet begins to brown slightly but the top is moist.

If you're using a frying pan, cut partway through the omelet across the center and carefully turn one half over the other. The omelet pan makes it easy to flip one half over the other. Serves 4. Chopped ham may be mixed with the green pepper and onion if you wish.

PARTY CHEESE BALL**

Equipment you will need:
Bowl for mixing
Cutting board or chopping bowl
Sharp knife
Mixing spoon
Plastic film for wrapping

Ingredients:

Sharp cheddar cheese, shredded	285 g (about 10 oz.)
Whipped cream cheese	2 packages, 230 g (about 8 oz.) each
Processed cheese spread	1 small jar (142 g or 5 oz.)
Onion or scallions, chopped	30 mL
Green pepper, chopped	30 mL
Worcestershire sauce	30 mL
Pinch of salt	
Pecan bits or chopped parsley	

Let the cheddar cheese warm in the kitchen for a while so that it is room temperature when you begin. Combine with the other cheeses, onion, green pepper, Worcestershire sauce, and salt. Mix it all together until it is thoroughly blended. Now, be sure your hands are very clean because you will have to use them to do this. Form the cheeses into a ball. Roll the whole thing in the chopped pecans or parsley or whatever you have chosen; chopped watercress or even toasted almonds may be used. Wrap in plastic film and chill several hours in the refrigerator. Serve on a plate or cheese board surrounded by crisp crackers. Use a small knife for spreading.

If only part of your cheese ball is eaten the first time you serve it, just form it into a smaller ball, rewrap it, and serve it again. A cheese ball keeps well in the refrigerator. It makes a super snack and a fine appetizer for a party.

HOLE-IN-ONE EGG BREAKFAST*

Equipment you will need:
Frying pan, 20 cm or larger
Wide plastic spatula
Juice glass for a cutter
Saucer
Tongs

Ingredients:

Butter or margarine	15 mL for each serving
Bread, preferably whole wheat	1 slice for each serving
Eggs	1 for each serving
Bacon	2 strips for each serving
Salt and pepper	

This is a quick and good breakfast. Heat half the butter in a frying pan. Cut the center out of a slice of bread using your juice glass.

Place the slice of bread in the frying pan and brown it on one side. Add the rest of the butter to the pan and turn the bread over. Break the egg in a saucer and gently slide it into the hole. Cook over low heat until done.

Have you seen your mother cooking bacon in the oven? It's easy. Lay the strips on the rack inside the broiler tray and put them under the broiler while you are cooking the eggs. Both should be finished about the same time. Bacon and eggs are both quick cookers, so keep a close watch. Of course, if it's just you, making your own breakfast, you wouldn't bother turning on the oven. It would save energy to cook the bacon in the frying pan before you cook your Hole-in-One Breakfast. Two strips of bacon are about right for one person, so lay them flat in the pan and turn on medium heat. Be very careful of hot grease. Don't get too close to it. When the bacon is brown on one side, carefully turn it with your tongs. When crisp, turn off the heat and with your tongs lift it onto a plate covered with paper towel so that it will drain. With a potholder lift the frying pan off the burner onto a heat-proof mat and let it cool for a few minutes. Then pour off the hot grease into a metal cup and proceed with the cooking of your Hole-in-One Breakfast.

With a glass of milk and some fruit juice, you will have a good breakfast.

Continue moving the pan back and forth across the burner until you don't hear any more popping. Remove from the burner immediately, but continue shaking until no more pops are heard.

You should have about 2.5 L popped corn. Add the butter or margarine and the salt. Stir until well coated. Transfer to serving bowls and eat and eat and eat.

Oven Caramel Corn

You will also need a cake-type baking pan or casserole at least 25 x 25 cm (10 x 10 in.).

Ingredients:

Butter or margarine	125 mL
Brown sugar, packed	125 mL
Shelled pecans or almonds	125 mL
Shredded coconut	125 mL
Popped unsalted, unbuttered corn	1.5 L

Preheat the oven to 175 degrees C (350 F). Cream the butter and sugar together until fluffy. Mix the nuts and coconut with the popped corn, and add the butter and sugar mixture in several lumps. Heat in the oven 5 minutes. Take out, stir, and return to the oven 10 minutes more. Serve to your friends in bowls.

OVEN-SCRAMBLED EGGS**

Equipment you will need:
Casserole, about 2 L
Egg beater
Medium-sized bowl
Medium-sized saucepan
Fork

Ingredients:

Milk	300 mL
Eggs	12
Salt	5 mL
Butter or margarine	60 mL

Here's a special breakfast dish for Sunday morning, for Mother's Day, or for Christmas morning. It doesn't take much scrambling, but use a timer if you have one. When it's time to "fluff" the eggs, ask a grownup to help. Wear oven mitts.

Scald the milk. Watch it carefully because it will boil over easily. Break the eggs into a bowl and beat until they are all one color. Beat in the salt and carefully add the hot milk. Pour into the casserole and add the piece of butter, whole.

Bake at 175 degrees C (350 F) for 15 minutes. Remove from the oven and put on a heat-proof mat. Then carefully fluff or stir lightly with a fork and return to the oven. Bake 10 minutes more. Serves 8–10 people. If your family is smaller, cut the recipe in half and decrease the baking time about 5 minutes.

You can make this breakfast in half an hour if you ask someone to make the toast and pour the fruit juice and the milk. Let the grownups make the coffee.

POPCORN**

Equipment you will need:

Corn popper (preferred) or a large heavy skillet or saucepan with a side handle, about 25 cm. Must have a tight-fitting cover with a vent

Mixing spoon
Big bowl
Oven mitts

Buttered Popcorn

Ingredients:

Salad or popping oil (do not use butter or margarine for popping)	60 mL
Unpopped corn	125 mL
Butter or margarine	40 mL (more or less to taste)
Salt	2–3 mL

Popcorn was invented by the Indians, who thought certain kinds of corn had little demons in the kernels. The little demons made the popcorn pop or explode on hot rocks. Of course we know it isn't little demons at all but moisture inside that makes the corn pop.

Be sure to use potholders or oven mitts. If you have a commercial corn popper, follow the directions on the popper. If you are using your own saucepan or skillet with a vent in the cover, be extra careful because the pan will be hot. You may need some adult help.

Heat the oil. When three or four kernels of corn spin in the oil, add the rest of the corn, covering the bottom of the pan. Put on the lid.

Begin shaking the pan a little on the burner to keep the corn moving in the oil. You will hear a popping inside the pan. The vent should be open.

FRENCH TOAST*

Equipment you will need:
Big frying pan or a nonstick cookie sheet
Wide plastic spatula
Shallow pan or bowl
Fork or wire whisk

Ingredients:	
Eggs	2
Milk	100 mL
Salt	1 mL
Pinch of pepper	
Slices of bread	4
Butter or margarine	30 mL

Beat the eggs, milk, salt, and pepper right in the bowl or pan where you will soak the bread. Any kind of bread is good for French Toast, but this is a good way to use up the slices at the end of the whole wheat loaf that are just a little bit stale.

Float the bread slices, one or two at a time, in the milk and egg mixture. Turn the slice over and soak the other side, too.

If you are using the frying pan method, heat it with half the butter until it bubbles. Put in two slices of bread. When they are brown on one side, turn them over, using the spatula, and brown them on the other side. Be sure the heat is not too high or your toast will burn.

If you are using the oven method, preheat the oven to 200 degrees C (400 F) with the cookie sheet in it. Remove the hot cookie sheet (be sure to use hot mitts or a potholder) and put it on a heat-proof mat. Place the soaked bread on the cookie sheet and bake about 5 minutes. Then take the cookie sheet out of the oven, turn the bread over, and bake 5 minutes more until it is brown and crisp around the edges. This is an easy way to make French Toast for the family so it will be all ready at once.

Serve with maple syrup or jam.

For crispier French Toast, add 15 mL maple syrup to the egg batter.

If you like French Toast for lunch, you will want something crunchy to go with it. Peel and wash a raw carrot or scrub some celery to go with the toast. Drink a glass of milk, too, to make it a balanced meal. Eat an apple or some other fruit for dessert.

VEGETABLE SNACKER DIP*

Equipment you will need:
Sharp knife
Vegetable peeler
Medium-sized mixing bowl

Ingredients:

Dairy sour cream	250 mL
Mayonnaise	250 mL
Onions, dry or fresh, minced	30 mL
Dill weed, dried	5 mL
Celery salt	1 mL
Onion salt	1 mL
Pinch of sugar	
Several kinds of vegetables, such as carrots, green pepper, cucumber, radishes, cauliflower, celery	

Mix the first seven ingredients together and refrigerate while you get the vegetables ready.

Wash and scrape some carrots and cut into sticks. Do the same with celery. Radishes and cauliflower can be washed and the cauliflower separated into bite-size pieces. Maybe you have some favorite raw vegetable to try.

Serve the fresh vegetables on a tray with a bowl of Snacker Dip in the center.

Try it as an after-school snack for your Scout troop. Your mother might even borrow the recipe for company appetizers if she finds out how good it is.

CHEESE GRITS**

Equipment you will need:
Large saucepan
Stirring spoon
Grater or cutting board
Sharp knife
Casserole, 2 L, any shape

Ingredients:	
Boiling water	1 L
Salt	5 mL
Instant grits	250 mL
Margarine or butter	1 stick, about 125 mL
Sharp cheddar cheese, grated or cut in small pieces	250 mL
Eggs	2
Milk	

Bring salted water to a rolling boil and slowly stir in the grits. Be careful of the steam. Cook three minutes, stirring constantly. Remove from the heat, put on a heat-proof mat, and stir in the margarine and cheese. Break the eggs into a 250 mL measure and add enough milk to make 250 mL. Add to the grits, stirring vigorously.

Grease the casserole with a little butter, pour in the mixture, and bake 45 minutes to one hour at 175 degrees C (350 F). Makes 6–8 servings.

For a special treat: Bake the night before in a square pan. Store overnight in the refrigerator. The next morning, cut in squares and roll lightly in flour. Then brown on all sides in a frying pan, using a little butter or margarine. Serve the squares with maple syrup while still warm. This is a very special dish, but you will also need fruit and milk to make it a breakfast good for you, too.

Let's Have
a Party

Lunch Break
and Suppertime

Beat the eggs in a bowl. Add the milk and water to the beaten eggs. Still beating, gradually add the flour and stir hard until the batter is smooth. Add the melted butter, sugar, and vanilla. The batter will look like thick yellow cream.

Have your frying pan hot enough so a drop of water bounces and evaporates on it. Dip your 25 mL measure into the batter and empty it into the hot pan, tilting to spread it evenly. Turn the heat down and cook until the top is dry and the edges are just browned. Adjust the heat for each new crepe. Lift out with a wide flexible spatula and turn onto a plate. Repeat, stacking the crepes brown side up. This is so that the filling, when rolled inside, will not soak through. Makes 14 crepes.

To serve, plan on about two crepes per person. First put a spoonful of custard in the center of each crepe. Add a spoonful of blueberry sauce and roll seam side down. Add more sauce on top and a dab of non-dairy topping, then a few berries for garnish. Peaches instead of blueberries make delicious crepes, too.

Crepes don't always have to be dessert. You could leave out the sugar and fill them with any number of meat or vegetable sauces. Invent your own combinations after you have mastered the art of making crepes.

AMERICANESE SPAGHETTI**

Equipment you will need:
Large saucepan
Medium-sized frying pan
Medium-sized casserole, about 2 L
Cutting board
Paring knife
Colander

Ingredients:

Ground beef	250 mL (280 g, about ½ lb.)
Green pepper, chopped	½
Onion, small, minced	1
Salt	
Elbow spaghetti, uncooked	250 mL (about 235 g)
Tomato soup, undiluted	1 can (305 g)
Parmesan cheese or grated Italian cheese	25 mL or more for top

In the frying pan, brown the meat, green pepper, and onion. Sprinkle a little salt in the pan to help prevent sticking.

Add spaghetti to 1.5 L salted boiling water in the saucepan. Turn down the heat and cook until just tender. The water should just simmer without boiling over. Or follow the directions on the package. Drain by pouring the spaghetti into a colander in the sink.

Combine the spaghetti and meat mixture in the casserole. Stir in the undiluted tomato soup. Sprinkle generously with Parmesan cheese or grated Italian cheese. Bake at 175 C (350 F) for 30 minutes. Serves 4–6.

Blueberry Crepes are something spectacular and really show your skill in cooking. There are three things to make—a custard, a sauce, and the crepes themselves. It's the crepes that are the hardest. They take a light touch to turn out delicate and thin.

The good news is that you don't have to make everything at once. You can make all three things ahead and store them in the refrigerator, even overnight.

First, make the custard. That's easy. Just follow the directions on the pudding package, cool, and store in the refrigerator.

Next make the Blueberry Sauce. Mix the cornstarch and sugar, add water and corn syrup, then lemon juice. Bring to a boil, stirring. Add one pint of blueberries and return to a boil. (Save the second pint of blueberries for topping.) Remove the sauce from the heat and set aside or refrigerate.

Now for the crepes. The small frying pan will help you keep the crepes all one size. You should get about 14 crepes from this recipe. If you have a crepe pan, follow the directions on it. Wipe the inside of the frying pan with a small amount of salad oil.

PEET-ZA!**

Equipment you will need:
Pizza pan, about 33 cm (13 in.)
Mixing bowl
Wooden stirring spoon
Rolling pin
Sifter
Paring knife

Ingredients:

Flour	375 mL
Salt	2 mL
Baking powder	1 mL
Sugar	5 mL
Dry yeast	1 small packet
Warm water	175 mL

Sift the flour, salt, baking powder, and sugar together in a bowl and add the dry yeast. Mix the yeast in very well. Add the warm water and stir until it is well mixed and it forms a lump.

Turn out on a lightly floured board or the clean counter top. Invert the bowl over the dough and let rest 5 minutes.

Knead as you would for bread (see page 94) about 5 minutes or until the dough is smooth. Roll out and carefully lift into the pizza pan. Press into the pan and trim the edge. The crust could be made ahead if you wish, and stored in the refrigerator until your friends are ready.

Filling

Preheat oven to 220 degrees C (425 F).
Ingredients:

Tomato sauce	1 can, about 300 mL (8 oz.)
Italian seasoning	10 mL (or a little more)
Onion, sliced or chopped	50 mL
Green pepper, sliced	½
Summer sausage, peeled and quartered, *or*	4 slices (16 pieces)
Ground beef	16–18 small balls (about 250 mL)
Mozzarella cheese, shredded	250 mL
Parmesan cheese for topping	

Spread the tomato sauce evenly over the crust and sprinkle with Italian seasoning, or mix seasoning with tomato sauce before spreading. Arrange the onion, green pepper, sausage, Mozzarella cheese, and Parmesan cheese, in that order, on the tomato sauce. Other things may be added such as black olive slices or mushrooms. Use your imagination to make your own special pizza! Bake at 220 degrees C (425 F) 10–15 minutes or until the cheese bubbles and the crust is golden brown at the edge. Serve hot. Two people could eat it all, or it could serve 5–6. It depends on how much you like pizza.

BLUEBERRY CREPES***

The Custard

Equipment you will need:	Ingredients:	
Medium-sized saucepan	Plain vanilla pudding	
Stirring spoon	(not instant)	1 box (about 105 g)
Bowl for storing in refrigerator	Milk	500 mL

The Blueberry Sauce

Equipment you will need:	Ingredients:	
Saucepan, about 2 L	Cornstarch	18 mL
Stirring spoon	Sugar	125 mL
Bowl for storing the sauce	Water	50 mL
	White corn syrup	50 mL
	Lemon juice	10 mL
	Fresh or frozen blueberries	
	(save half for later)	1 L (about 2 pints)
	Non-dairy topping	500 mL or more

The Crepes

Equipment you will need:	Ingredients:	
Small frying pan	Salad oil	
Fork or wire whisk	Eggs, beaten	2
Medium-sized mixing bowl	Milk	75 mL
Plate for stacking crepes	Water	75 mL
Spatula, wide flexible metal or plastic	Flour, sifted	180 mL
Small pan for melting	Butter or margarine, melted	15 mL
	Sugar	30 mL
	Vanilla	5 mL

SCOTT AND BILLY'S GET-TOGETHERS*

Equipment you will need:
Aluminum foil, 30 cm wide
Paring knife

Ingredients:

Ground beef	125 mL (140 g, about ¼ lb.) per person
Potato, cut up	½
or	
Instant fortified rice	15 mL
Raw onion rings	2
Carrot, sliced	1
Tomato wedge	1
Salt and pepper	

For each person, tear off two squares of aluminum foil and put one on top of the other. Form a hamburger patty in the center of the foil. On top of the patty place the potato slices or the rice. Add onion, carrot, tomato, and plenty of salt and pepper. Fold opposite sides of the foil together and seal all the way around to make a leak-proof packet.

These delicious little dinners take about one hour on a very hot grill or in a 200-degree C (400 F) oven. Serves one.

Get-togethers are great for camping. You could make them in the morning, refrigerate, and go swimming. Then grill them for supper. Allow a little extra time if they are cold.

Try some crunchy French bread and butter as a "go-with," and maybe a jar of chocolate pudding and milk from your Thermos for dessert.

out one part on a flour-sprinkled board or pastry cloth with a rolling pin. Keep the unused parts in the refrigerator until you are ready to use them. Roll the dough out to about 3 mm (⅛ in.) in thickness. Cut out with cookie cutters. One-third of the dough will make about 2 dozen cookies.

Preheat the oven to 190 degrees C (375 F) and bake the cookies 6–8 minutes on a greased cookie sheet. Cool on racks. Bake the other batches in the same way. These cookies need a bit of frosting to bring out the mild ginger flavor.

Butter Icing*

Equipment you will need:
Medium-sized mixing bowl
Stirring spoon
Sifter
Spreading knife

Ingredients:

Butter or margarine, softened	60 mL
Confectioners sugar, sifted	500 mL
Milk	15 mL
Vanilla	2 mL

Cream the butter or margarine and sugar together until well blended. Gradually add the milk and vanilla and stir until smooth.

When cookies are cool, frost them with the icing.

CHEESE SOUFFLÉ**

Equipment you will need:
Medium-sized casserole
Larger pan into which casserole will fit
Bowl for mixing, about 1½ or 2 L
Egg beater
Paring knife

Ingredients:

Bread, crusts removed	4 slices
Sharp cheddar cheese, grated	175 mL
Eggs, beaten	4 large
Milk	500 mL
Dry mustard	1 mL
Cooking sherry (if your mother says	
it's all right)	25 mL
Salt	1 mL
Pinch of pepper	

Your mother is having some friends for lunch. If you try this cheese soufflé for your family first, then *maybe* she will let you make it the night before or several hours ahead of her party.

Cut the crusts off the bread and dice the remainder. Save the crusts to use for a buttered crumb topping for another recipe. Butter the casserole and alternate layers of bread with grated cheese. Mix the beaten eggs with the milk, salt, pepper, mustard, and sherry. Pour over the bread and cheese. Refrigerate, covered, overnight or at least two hours.

About 30–40 minutes before baking, take the casserole out of the refrigerator so it will be at room temperature.

A little more than an hour before mealtime, preheat the oven to 175 C (350 F). Set the soufflé in a larger pan with about two centimeters of warm water in it. Bake for 50–60 minutes. A few minutes before serving, remove from the oven. The two pans can be hard to lift, so get adult help if necessary. Take the soufflé out of the larger pan. Bake it by itself 5 minutes to be sure the soufflé is done on the bottom.

Serve it with a green salad, rolls, and a fruit dessert for a lovely luncheon. That's fancier than a lunch. Serves 4.

GINGER PEOPLE***

Equipment you will need:
Big mixing bowl
Mixing spoon (an electric mixer would be helpful
   but not necessary)
Sifter
Cookie cutters, ginger boy shape and others
Rolling pin
Pastry cloth or board (helpful)
Cookie sheets

Ingredients:

Butter or margarine	1 stick (about 125 mL)
Brown sugar, firmly packed	180 mL
Large egg	1
Molasses	80 mL
Flour	565 mL
Baking soda	5 mL
Salt	5 mL
Cinnamon	10 mL
Ginger	5 mL
Nutmeg	2 mL

These cookies take a little time to mix and bake. You may want to bake them one day and decorate them the next.

Mix the butter or margarine, sugar, and egg together until light and fluffy. Add the molasses.

Sift the flour with the soda, salt, cinnamon, ginger, and nutmeg into the mixture and stir until everything is well blended. It makes a stiff dough. Refrigerate until the dough is cold (at least one hour).

Divide the dough into three parts and roll

RANGE-TOP CHILI**

Equipment you will need:
Dutch oven
Cutting board
Sharp knife
Large frying pan
Wooden spoon

Ingredients:

Ground beef	750 mL (840 g, about 1¾ lbs.)
Celery, cut fine	3 stalks
Onion, cut fine	1 medium
Green pepper, cut fine	1
Canned tomatoes	1 can (about 820 g)
Red kidney beans	1 can (about 820 g)
Water	250 mL
Salt	5 mL
Chili powder	6 mL
Seasoned salt	5 mL
Condensed tomato soup	½ a 305-g can, if needed

Brown the ground beef in the frying pan. A little salt sprinkled in the pan helps keep the meat from sticking. Mix all the ingredients in the Dutch oven except the tomato soup. Reserve the soup until the end. If the tomatoes are whole, cut them up first. Bring the chili to a boil, then turn the burner to low and stir the mixture well. Put the cover on and allow to simmer for one hour. Stir it occasionally.

After one hour check your chili for taste. Stir it, then take out a spoonful, cool it a bit, and taste it. Does it need salt? If so, add a little. Is it too thin? If so, add the tomato soup and stir it in. Then leave the cover off for the next hour of cooking to reduce the liquid. Watch it carefully. Taste again. It should be ready to eat.

Serve in individual bowls with saltine crackers. A green salad is a good side dish. You might have time to make Confederate Pears (page 76) for dessert. That would make a delicious supper on a cold day. Serves 4–6.

HAND-MADE COOKIES*

Equipment you will need:
Medium-sized mixing bowl
Mixing spoon
Cookie sheet
Sifter

Ingredients:

Flour	500 mL
Confectioners sugar	250 mL
Margarine or butter	2 sticks (about 230 g)
Vanilla	5 mL
Salt	1 mL
Nuts, dates, or raisins	
finely chopped	125 mL
Granulated sugar	50 mL

Even your young brother or sister can help make these cookies. You don't cut them or drop them from a spoon or slice them. To make them, you just squeeze them in your fist. They could be round or just fist-shaped. Wash your hands first!

Sift the flour and confectioners sugar together. Cut the margarine or butter into small pieces and mix with the flour, sugar, vanilla, and salt. When the mixture looks like coarse sand, stir in the nuts or dates or raisins. Mold the cookies in your hand, packing the dough, which will seem dry. Pack it tight. Roll the cookies in the granulated sugar and place on the cookie sheet.

Bake 20–25 minutes at 175 degrees C (350 F) or until slightly browned on the edges. Makes about 28–36 cookies, depending on the size.

ORIENTAL SKILLET SUPPER***

Equipment you will need:
Large frying pan or wok
Sharp knife for meat slicing
Cutting board
Paring knife
Small mixing bowl

Ingredients:

Lean beef cut into strips	280 g (just over ½ lb.)
Salad oil	30 mL
Onion, sliced	1
Green pepper, sliced	1
Celery, sliced	250 mL
Green beans, slivered	250 mL
Mushrooms, sliced	1 small can
Water	65 mL
Cornstarch	20 mL
Soy sauce	15 mL

It might be a good idea to ask someone to help you slice the meat for this dish. It must be very thin.

Brown the meat quickly in the hot frying pan with the oil. Add the vegetables and cook 3–5 minutes, or even less if you like your vegetables really crisp.

Mix the water, cornstarch, and soy sauce in the small bowl and stir until smooth. Add to the meat and vegetables and cook 10 minutes, stirring until the liquid is clear and shiny and the beans are just tender-crisp. Salt to taste and serve with cooked rice. Pass more soy sauce, which people may add if they wish. With a glass of milk and a sweet dessert, it's a perfect meal.

The trick with Oriental cookery is having everything ready. Have the table set, the milk poured, the rice cooked, and your vegetables and meat all cut up. Then begin cooking the Skillet Supper. Serves 4.

IMPOSSIBLE PIE**

Equipment you will need:
Glass pie plate, 25 cm (about 10 in.)
Medium-sized mixing bowl
Egg beater or electric blender

Ingredients:

Eggs	4
Milk	500 mL
Sugar	125 mL
Butter, melted	45 mL
Prepared biscuit mix	125 mL
Vanilla	5 mL

Preheat the oven to 200 degrees C (400 F). Break the eggs into the bowl and beat them well. Add the milk, sugar, butter, and biscuit mix. Beat well. Stir in the vanilla. Pour the mixture into a greased glass pie plate. Bake 25–30 minutes or until the top is just brown.

This pie wiggles while it bakes. If you are lucky enough to have a window in your oven, you will see it breathe, then grow and swell, and finally collapse as it cooks. Quite a show! Serves 6.

When the pie is baked, the crust will be on top. Cool it and serve plain or top with fruit.

Maybe you can think of some ways to make this a "possible" pie. You will find it is very good alone, but you could dress it up by making a graham cracker crust for it (page 77) and putting a spoonful of cherry pie filling on top of each piece for an elegant dessert.

THE GREAT AMERICAN MEAT LOAF AND POTATO DINNER**

Equipment you will need:
Bread or meat loaf pan 13 x 24 cm
  (this is a regular bread pan)
Small bowl
Medium-sized bowl
Paring knife
Kitchen fork

Ingredients:

Leftover bread	2 slices
Milk	125 mL
Eggs	2
Salt	2 mL
Pinch of pepper	
Ground beef	875 mL (980 g, about 2 lbs.)
Onion, minced	15 mL
Catsup	25 mL or more

Wash your hands, please! This is very important. In the medium-sized bowl, break up the bread and soak it in half of the milk. When soft, tear it into pieces the size of nickels. Open the eggs into the small bowl and beat them with the fork until they are all one color. Then add the rest of the milk and salt and pepper. Add the ground beef, the onion, and the catsup to the bread and mix well. Then pour the egg mixture into it.

Hands very clean? Start mixing with your hands. It is *very* squishy. Mix until everything is well blended, then turn it into the bread pan. Pat it down and bake one hour at 200 degrees C (400 F). Serves 6 or 8 depending on how thin you slice it.

Baked Potatoes*

These go right in the oven with the Meat Loaf. Select one potato for each eater. Scrub each potato with a brush. Poke the fork into each one twice. This will let the steam out while it is baking. Bake one hour in the oven on the rack next to the meat.

When you are ready to serve, wearing your oven mitts, cut a big crisscross in each potato with the paring knife. Put in a big pat of butter or serve with sour cream at the table.

This dinner needs a vegetable and a salad to make it balance. Zucchini Bake (page 69) or Green Beans (page 70) and a fruit salad would be good. With your usual milk, you might not want any dessert.

PAPER BAG APPLE PIE**

Equipment you will need:
Paring knife
Paper bag
Aluminum foil

Ingredients:

A baked crumb crust (see page 77)	
Large cooking apples	4–6 (about 1½ L sliced)
Flour	30 mL
Sugar	200 mL
Nutmeg	3 mL
Cinnamon	3 mL
Butter or margarine, soft	15 mL

You won't need a bowl for mixing. All you really need is the crumb crust and your metric measures. You will have a paper bag and foil on hand anyway.

Preheat oven to 200 degrees C (400 F). Wash and peel the apples and slice the easy way. Hold the peeled apple over the paper bag, cut thin slices from it, and let them fall right into the bag. Keep turning the apple so that you cut it evenly all around and are left with only the core, which you can then throw out. Put the flour-sugar-nutmeg-cinnamon mixture into the paper bag with the apple slices. Shake until all are completely coated. Lift the apple slices into the baked crumb crust and spread the rest of the flour-sugar-nutmeg-cinnamon mixture evenly over the apples. Dot with butter and cover with foil, tucking it carefully around the edges but not too tightly.

Bake for 45 minutes at the center of your oven. Remove and allow to cool with the foil still on. Cut in 8 pieces. Serve with a scoop of vanilla ice cream.

SWIMMIN' CHICKEN**

Equipment you will need:
Covered casserole suitable for oven or range top,
   2- or 3-L capacity
Paper or plastic bag
Small bowl or cup
Wooden mixing spoon

Ingredients:	
Flour	65 mL
Salt	2 mL
Dash of black pepper	
Paprika	1 mL
Frying chicken, cut up	1
Butter, melted	30 mL
Milk	250 mL
Parsley, chopped	30 mL

Put 50 mL of flour in a paper or plastic bag. Add salt, pepper, and paprika. Wash and dry the chicken pieces and take out any pin feathers. Shake the chicken pieces in the sack, one or two pieces at a time, until well coated. Place in the casserole, skin side up, and drizzle melted butter over all. Save any flour mixture that is left for making sauce or gravy later.

Bake in the oven at 200 degrees C (400 F) one hour. Cover for the first 45 minutes, then remove the cover. When done, remove the chicken to a platter and cover to keep hot.

In the small bowl mix 15 mL of flour with the flour you have saved. Add a little of the milk and stir until free of lumps. Add the rest of the milk, then transfer to casserole in which the chicken was baked. Heat slowly on top of the range, scraping the sides and bottom of the pan with a wooden spoon to loosen the meat drippings and stirring constantly until the mixture thickens into a smooth gravy. Add salt to taste. It may need a bit more.

Serve the gravy over the hot chicken with a little chopped parsley for garnish. It's very good with black-eyed peas or baked beans. Also goes well with rice and a fresh vegetable salad (see page 55). A bran muffin and a glass of milk would be good too. Serves 4–6.

GRAHAM CRACKER CRUST AND YOGURT PIE*

Equipment you will need:
Pie pan, 23 cm (about 9 in.)
Rolling pin
Mixing bowl
Mixing spoon or spatula
Small pan for melting butter or margarine

Ingredients:

Graham crackers, crushed   250 mL (about 12–14 crackers)

Butter or margarine, melted   30 mL

Crush the graham crackers with the rolling pin into crumbs a little coarser than cornmeal. Measure into a bowl. Add the melted butter and mix very well. Press mixture evenly in the bottom and around the sides of a greased pie pan. Bake 5 minutes, or until just browned, in a preheated oven at 190 degrees C (375 F). Cool the pie crust.

Peach Yogurt Filling

Equipment you will need:
Large mixing bowl
Mixing spoon
Paring knife

Ingredients:

Non-dairy topping   1 medium-sized tub (255 g)

Peach yogurt   2 cartons, 227 g each

Fresh peaches   2 or 3

Mix the topping and the yogurt. Spread it evenly in the cooled graham cracker crust and chill. Just before serving, cover the top with sliced peaches. You may sweeten the peaches with 15 mL sugar if you wish. Serves 8. Try it with strawberries and strawberry yogurt, too.

BARBECUED RIBS AND SAUCE**

Equipment you will need:
Large kettle
Large shallow baking pan or the bottom of your
    broiler pan
Sharp knife

Ingredients:
Spareribs	454 g per person
	(about 1 lb.)
Bay leaf	1
Barbecue sauce, already made	
(see recipe below)	

Barbecued ribs are finger food. They're fun to eat, easy to cook, and great with black-eyed peas and a big tossed salad of greens. Make the sauce the day before if you want to cut down on cooking time. You could also mix it up while the ribs are boiling slowly in the big kettle.

Ask the butcher to crack the ribs in the middle, or buy the small ribs. Cut ribs into serving-size portions by cutting down between the ribs, leaving three or four ribs in each piece.

Two hours before the meal, in the big kettle, begin to cook the ribs. Cover them with water, add a bay leaf, and bring them to a boil. Lower the heat so the water just keeps boiling, and cook, covered, about 45 minutes.

Preheat the oven to 175 degrees C (350 F) and transfer the ribs to a shallow baking pan. Spread with barbecue sauce and bake uncovered 45 minutes. Add more barbecue sauce and bake 10 minutes more. They should be tender and juicy and just a little bit browned.

Sauce for Ribs and Frank-'n'-Bobs*

Equipment you will need:
Reusable glass jar, about 300 mL

Ingredients:		Double
Prepared mustard	5 mL	10 mL
Catsup	125 mL	250 mL
Honey	75 mL	150 mL
Unsweetened pineapple juice	75 mL	150 mL
Soy sauce	3 mL	6 mL

This sauce can be made ahead and stored in the refrigerator. Measure it right into a reusable glass jar with a tight cover, such as a peanut-butter jar. The recipe makes almost 300 mL and fills the jar. Use it on ribs and on Frank-'n'-Bobs. Maybe you can think of some other uses for it.

Combine the mustard and catsup and mix well. Add the honey, pineapple juice, and soy sauce and stir until well blended.

CONFEDERATE PEARS*

Equipment you will need:
Shallow rectangular baking dish, about 18 x 28 cm
   (7 x 11 in.)
Cutting board or sheet of waxed paper
Rolling pin

Ingredients:

Butter, melted	15 mL
Pear halves, drained	6
Orange juice	30 mL
Raisins, seedless	15 mL
Coconut macaroons, crushed	250 mL (about 20–22 cookies)
Brown sugar	15 mL
Heavy cream, whipped	125 mL plus 15 mL powdered sugar
or non-dairy topping	125 mL

Preheat the oven to 160 degrees C (325 F). Melt the butter in the baking dish in the oven while you get out the rest of the ingredients. Then take the dish out of the oven and place the pears in it. Sprinkle with orange juice, raisins, crumbled macaroons (a rolling pin will do the trick), and brown sugar. Bake 15 minutes. Serve warm with the whipped cream mixed with powdered sugar or with non-dairy topping. Serves 6.

FRANK-'n'-BOBS**

Equipment you will need:
Skewers, if possible, or long trussing pins for
    poultry, or aluminum foil
Paring knife
Cutting board
Small saucepan
Tongs
Spoon

Ingredients:

Wieners	1 or 2 for each person
Green peppers, cut in squares	1 or 2 large
Miniature tomatoes or firm regular tomato wedges	several
Crushed pineapple	1 #1 can (234 g)

These are assembled on skewers like shish-kebabs. Cut wieners in pieces about 3 cm long (that's about an inch). Alternate on skewers with green pepper and tomato pieces.

If you don't have skewers, try using the long pins your mother uses to close the hole in the Thanksgiving turkey. Or make little boats of aluminum foil. Pinch the corners and alternate the pieces in a boat as you would on a skewer. Make a boat for everybody in the family.

If you are using skewers, lay them flat in the broiler pan and drizzle some of the crushed pineapple over each. Then spoon on the sauce (page 45). Now is the time to turn on the broiler to 260 degrees C (500 F). Broil 5 minutes. Using oven mitts, place on a heat-proof mat. With tongs, turn and spoon on more sauce. Return to the oven 5 more minutes or until slightly brown. Watch carefully.

Good with a baked potato and a big green salad, whole wheat bread and a glass of milk.

SNOWBALLS**

Equipment you will need:
Tray or cookie sheet with an edge
Rectangular cake pan large enough for the number
  of snowballs you plan to make
Waxed paper
Rubber plate scraper

Ingredients:

Vanilla or brown edge wafers,	
about 6.5 cm in diameter	1 box (about 40
(2½ in.)	wafers)
Non-dairy topping	1 tub
or heavy cream, whipped	250 mL (about ½
	pint)
Sweetened crushed	1 can, 234 g
pineapple, drained	(about 8¼ oz.)
Moist shredded coconut	100 g (about 3½ oz.)

Lay the waxed paper in the bottom of the cookie sheet and use this as a working surface. Have the cake pan ready. Begin by frosting the top of a wafer with whipped cream or non-dairy topping, using the rubber plate scraper. Add 2 mL drained pineapple to the top. Stack a second wafer on top of the first, frost it, and add pineapple. Stack four wafers this way, but don't frost the top one.

When four are stacked, carefully frost the sides. Sprinkle coconut on the waxed paper and gently roll the stacked wafers in it. Now frost the top, sprinkle with coconut, and set aside in the cake pan. As soon as you have several snowballs made, put the cake pan in the refrigerator and continue making the snowballs.

It takes four wafers for each snowball, so read the label on the box and buy enough to make the number you want. Snowballs should be chilled for several hours before serving. They're beautiful and delicious, too.

You might want to try making snowballs with chocolate wafers.

BAKED CHOP SUEY**

Equipment you will need:
Large casserole, about 3 L
Medium-sized frying pan
Plastic or rubber spatula
Cutting board
Paring or slicing knife

Ingredients:

Ground beef	500 mL (560 g, about 1¼ lbs.)
Onion, chopped	500 mL
Condensed cream of chicken soup	1 can (305 g)
Condensed cream of mushroom soup	1 can (305 g)
Water	375 mL
Soy sauce	60 mL
Minute rice, uncooked	125 mL
Celery, chopped	250 mL
Canned Chinese noodles	250 mL

Brown the ground beef in the frying pan. Sprinkle the pan with a little salt first to keep the meat from sticking. Mix all the other ingredients except the Chinese noodles with the meat in the casserole. Bake, covered, about an hour and a half at 175 degrees C (350 F). For the last ten minutes of cooking, remove the cover and add the noodles on top. Serves 4–6.

This Baked Chop Suey could be very good served with Spinach Salad (page 52) or even Shimmy Salad (page 58). You might make brownies for dessert (page 74). There's no recipe for your glass of milk!

Note: Sometimes you can find chopped onions already packaged in the stores. Saves a lot of crying.

DOUBLE BROWNIES**

Equipment you will need:
Medium-sized cake pan 20 x 20 cm (about 8 in.
   square)
Mixing bowl
Mixing spoon
Sifter
Extra bowl or sheet of waxed paper for sifting
Egg beater or wire whisk

Ingredients:		Double
Eggs	2	4
Sugar	250 mL	500 mL
Cooking oil	125 mL	250 mL
Flour	150 mL	300 mL
Baking powder	2 mL	4 mL
Salt	2 mL	4 mL
Cocoa	100 mL	200 mL
Vanilla	5 mL	10 mL
Chopped nuts	200 mL	400 mL

Doubling metric is easy when you have a recipe as good as these brownies. One recipe makes a dozen, but you might like twice as many. Or three times as many!

Beat the eggs with the egg beater or wire whisk until frothy. Add the sugar, beating, then the oil, and mix well. Put the flour, baking powder, salt, and cocoa into the sifter. Sift into the egg-sugar-oil mixture and beat well. Add the vanilla and chopped nuts and stir in. Spread evenly in a greased pan.

Bake at 175 degrees C (350 F) 35–40 minutes or until a toothpick inserted in the center comes out clean. Cool slightly before cutting into squares.

If you double the recipe, you will need a larger baking pan, of course. And it will take a little more time to bake doubles or triples, but not twice as long. Use the toothpick test to tell when they are just right.

SEAFOOD CASSEROLE**

Equipment you will need:
Saucepan, about 2 L
Stirring spoon
Medium-sized casserole
Mixing bowl

Ingredients:

Butter or margarine	30 mL
Flour	30 mL
Milk	250 mL
Condensed cream of shrimp soup	1 can (305 g)
Sharp cheddar cheese, cut up or shredded	125 mL
Red salmon	1 can (454 g)
Frozen peas, slightly thawed	½ package (about 140 g)
Prepared biscuit mix	250 mL

Melt butter or margarine in a saucepan, add flour, and stir until lumps are gone. Slowly add the milk, stirring constantly until thick. Add the soup and heat until the mixture bubbles. Add the shredded cheese and gently stir in the salmon and peas. Transfer to the casserole. Bake at 160 degrees C (325 F) 45 minutes.

Prepare the biscuit mix in the mixing bowl according to directions on the package. Use 250 mL of the mix in place of one cup. Spoon eight dumpling-type biscuits on top of the hot casserole mixture and return to the oven. Bake 15 minutes more at 220 degrees C (425 F).

Serve with a green salad (page 55). Serves 4.

ERIC'S CAKE**

Equipment you will need:
Large rectangular cake pan 23 x 33 cm (9 x 12 in.)
Large mixing bowl
Small mixing bowl
Egg beater
Stirring spoon

Ingredients:

Instant chocolate pudding mix	1 package, 127 g (about 4½ oz.)
Yellow cake mix	1 package, 525 g
Large eggs	2
Milk	500 mL
Vanilla	5 mL
Topping of chocolate bits, marshmallows, chocolate-covered candies, or crushed chocolate bars	

Combine the pudding mix and cake mix in one bowl and stir together well. Break the eggs into the smaller bowl and beat until smooth. Add the milk and vanilla to the eggs and mix well, then pour gradually into the dry ingredients and beat until the lumps are gone.

Preheat the oven to 175 degrees C (350 F). Grease the cake pan and pour the batter into it. Decorate the top with the chocolate bits or candy bits, or whatever you have decided to use for topping. Bake 40 minutes or until a toothpick inserted in the center comes out clean. Makes 12 or more big pieces.

Eric got this recipe from his cousin Bruce and then gave it to me. It's an easy cake to make and excellent to eat.

REAL SWEDISH MEATBALLS***

Equipment you will need:
Medium-sized mixing bowl
Large frying pan
Wide plastic spatula, two if you have them
Mixing spoon or fork

Ingredients:

Ground pork	125 mL (140 g, about ¼ lb.)
Ground beef	500 mL (560 g, about 1¼ lbs.)
Salt	5 mL
Pepper	2 mL
Nutmeg	2 mL
Egg, slightly beaten	1 large
Cornstarch	45 mL
Water	200–250 mL
Shortening for frying	50 mL (more if needed)

Mix the pork and beef together, or ask the butcher to grind them together. Add the salt, pepper, nutmeg, and slightly beaten egg. Gradually add the cornstarch to meat mixture, mixing well. Slowly stir in the water a little at a time, until it is all absorbed by the meat and cornstarch.

Form into meatballs about the size of walnuts. You should have about 36.

Heat the shortening in the frying pan over low heat and brown the meatballs, a few at a time, turning them so they brown on all sides. Use the spatulas to help turn them. You may need some help with this. Be careful of the hot grease. When all are browned, put them in the frying pan, cover it, and simmer on low heat for one hour. Or transfer the meatballs to a casserole and bake, covered, in the oven at 175 degrees C (350 F) one hour.

You might cook boiled potatoes and a green vegetable such as asparagus or broccoli (see page 70). With the Confetti Cabbage Salad (page 53), you would have a real Swedish supper.

CRAZY CAKE AND FROSTING**

Equipment you will need:
Square cake pan, 23 x 23 cm (9 x 9 in.)
Sifter
Fork or rubber plate scraper
Mixing bowl and spoon
Small pan for melting margarine
Cooling rack

Ingredients:

Flour	375 mL
Sugar	250 mL
Cocoa	60 mL
Baking soda	5 mL
Salt	2 mL
Salad oil, room temperature	80 mL
Vanilla	5 mL
Vinegar, white	15 mL
Cold water	250 mL

Preheat the oven to 175 degrees C (350 F). Put all the dry ingredients into the sifter and sift into the cake pan. That includes the flour, sugar, cocoa, baking soda, and salt.

Make three holes in this dry mixture. Pour the salad oil into one hole, the vanilla into another, and the vinegar into the third.

Pour cold water over everything and stir with the plate scraper until the ingredients are well blended and the batter is smooth. Bake in the oven 30–35 minutes or until a toothpick inserted in the center comes out clean. While the cake is baking, make the frosting listed below, since it must be poured over the cake while hot.

Frosting

Ingredients:

Powdered sugar	500 mL
Cocoa	45 mL
Margarine, melted	125 mL
Vanilla	5 mL
Coffee (preferably decaffeinated) either left over or made from instant coffee	45 mL

Mix everything together in a bowl until well blended and there are no lumps. When the cake is baked, set pan on a rack, pour the frosting over the hot cake, and let it cool. Crazy!

You're going to love this crazy cake, especially if you are out of eggs because you won't need any. This cake breaks rules instead of eggs. Cut into 9 or 12 pieces.

Salad
Bar

Desserts That Finish First

TEXAS TACO SALAD**

Equipment you will need:
Large frying pan
2 large mixing bowls or one big family-type
   salad bowl
Individual bowls for garnishes
Cutting board
Sharp knife

Ingredients:	
Ground beef	750 mL (840 g, about 1¾ lbs.)
Salad oil	15 mL
French dressing, your favorite kind	100 mL
Onion, chopped	60 mL
Salt	2 mL
Pepper	1 mL
Lettuce, washed and finely shredded	½ head
Tomatoes, washed and diced	2
Radishes, washed and sliced	125 mL
Taco chips, slightly broken	1 package, 180 g (about 6½ oz.)

Separate Garnishes:	
Avocado, peeled, cubed	1
Natural cheddar cheese, shredded	250 mL
Pitted ripe olives, sliced	50 mL
Dairy sour cream	250 mL (about ½ pint)

Brown the meat in salad oil in the frying pan. Then turn off the heat and very carefully skim off the grease with a spoon into a metal can or cup. Mix the meat with half the French dressing and the onion, salt, and pepper in a bowl.

In another bowl combine the lettuce, tomatoes, and radishes and toss lightly with the remaining dressing.

On each plate place a few broken taco chips. Add the meat mixture, then the lettuce mixture. Pass the garnishes in individual bowls at the table. Or toss all the ingredients except the taco chips in a very large bowl. When ready to serve, add the taco chips.

Texas Taco Salad is a great dish to take to a pot-luck supper. If you do this, save the dressing and sour cream to add at the last minute.

If Texas Taco is your whole meal, it will serve 4–5 generously. If it's just the salad, there's enough for 10–12. Delicious!

SQUAW CORN*

Equipment you will need:
Small frying pan
Medium-sized saucepan
Kitchen scissors
Mixing spoon
Slotted spoon

Ingredients:

Bacon, cut fine	2 slices
Onion, chopped	25 mL
Cream-style or plain corn	1 can, 450 g (about 1 lb.)
Tomatoes	1 can, 450 g (about 1 lb.)
Salt to taste	
Sugar or honey	15 mL

Cut the bacon with scissors and fry until crisp. Turn off the heat and with your slotted spoon lift onto a plate covered with paper towel to drain. Pour off nearly all the drippings into a metal cup or old can. Put the frying pan back on the burner, turn the heat low, add the onion, and cook it until transparent. If you are using cream-style corn, combine the corn and tomatoes in a saucepan, and then add the sugar or honey and onion. Test for salt and add some if needed. Garnish with bacon.

If you are using regular corn, it should be drained before combining with the tomatoes. Cream-style corn will help thicken the tomatoes.

Squaw Corn is good with the Great American Meat Loaf and Potato Dinner (page 43). Serves 4–5.

COOKING GREEN VEGETABLES*

To cook a green vegetable such as asparagus, broccoli, or green beans, first wash it thoroughly. Cut off the woody part of the stems of broccoli and asparagus. Snip the ends of the beans. Boil just enough salted water to cover the vegetable. Carefully add the vegetable and bring back to a boil. Then lower the heat and cook until just tender, usually about 15 minutes. Test with a fork. The vegetable should be crispy, not mushy. Drain very carefully or ask for help. Serve with melted butter.

For frozen vegetables, follow the directions on the package because they usually have been partially cooked.

SPINACH SALAD*

Equipment you will need:
Kitchen scissors
Small frying pan
Slotted spoon
Colander
Large salad bowl

Ingredients:

Bacon, cut in small pieces	3 slices
Spinach	230 g (about ½ lb.). A bag from the supermarket is usually about 454 g, or 1 lb.
Sugar	30 mL
Vinegar	30 mL
Water	15 mL
Drippings from bacon	
Salt and pepper if you wish	
Mandarin orange sections	1 can, 315 g (optional)

This salad is best put together just before eating. The dressing should still be warm but not hot.

Cut the bacon into small pieces with the scissors and then fry the bits carefully in the frying pan. When the bacon is crisp, turn off the heat and lift the pieces with a slotted spoon onto a plate covered with paper towel to drain. Reserve the drippings.

Wash and pick over the spinach leaves, taking out the center stem and tearing the leaves into fork-size pieces. Drain the spinach in the colander and partially dry with paper towels or a clean kitchen towel.

Now add the sugar, vinegar, and water to the bacon drippings and heat, stirring, over low heat until the sugar is dissolved. Turn off the burner. Put the dried spinach leaves into a large salad bowl and pour the dressing over it. Season with salt and pepper if you wish. Add the bacon bits and toss until the leaves are coated. You may add a small can of drained mandarin orange sections if you wish. Serves 4.

ZUCCHINI BAKE*

Equipment you will need:
Shallow casserole, about 2 L
Cutting board
Cutting knife
Medium-sized saucepan
Slotted spoon or spatula

Ingredients:

Big zucchini squash, sliced in rounds	8 slices, each about 3 cm thick
Onion, grated	15 mL
Dash of black pepper	
Dash of salt	
Tomatoes, chopped, canned or fresh	250 mL
Parmesan cheese	25 mL
Bread crumbs, buttered, toasted	125 mL

Preheat the oven to 175 degrees C (350 F). Cook the zucchini 5 minutes in boiling salted water to cover. Lift out with a slotted spoon into a greased casserole. Add onion, pepper, salt, and tomatoes. Sprinkle with Parmesan cheese and bread crumbs (see instructions below). Bake 45 minutes. Serves 4.

For the bread-crumb topping, grate or crush leftover bread or trimmed crusts and brown slightly in a frying pan with a little butter or margarine.

KIMI'S HAWAIIAN SALAD*

Equipment you will need:
Serving bowl
Two forks

Ingredients:

Mandarin orange sections, drained	250 mL	(about 315 g)
Pineapple chunks, drained	250 mL	(about 200 g)
Coconut	50 mL	

Mix all together in a serving bowl, tossing lightly with two forks. Serve on a lettuce leaf or eat plain. Serves 4.

CONFETTI CABBAGE SALAD**

Equipment you will need:
Sharp knife
Cutting board or wooden chopping bowl
Salad bowl for mixing
Cup or bowl for dressing

Ingredients:

Cabbage, shredded	500 mL
Carrot, cut fine	1 small
Green pepper, chopped	1 small
Parsley, cut fine	10 mL

On a board, cut the cabbage from the head in thin slices. Be sure to throw away the inner core. If this is too hard, use a chopping knife in a wooden bowl. If you are using the first method, cut the cabbage crosswise into small pieces before measuring.

Mix the carrot, green pepper, and parsley with the cabbage and toss with the Creamy Salad Dressing (page 54). Serves 4.

BAKED ACORN SQUASH*

Equipment you will need:
Flat cake pan with edges, any size
Sharp knife
Spoon

Ingredients:

Acorn squash	½ per person
Water	125 mL
Butter or margarine	15 mL per person
Brown sugar	15 mL per person
Sprinkle of cinnamon	

An American vegetable that is easy to prepare, acorn squash is especially good in the fall when it is plentiful. Allow half a squash for each person; for small children, cut the piece in half after it is cooked.

Have someone help cut the squash in two crosswise. Scoop out the seeds. In a flat pan large enough for all the squash halves to lie flat on the bottom, turn them cut side down and add the water to the pan.

Bake one hour at 200 degrees C (400 F). When done, turn them over and in each center put 15 mL butter and 15 mL brown sugar. Sprinkle with a little cinnamon.

Serve with Swimmin' Chicken (page 44) and a fruit salad, if you wish—and a glass of milk, of course.

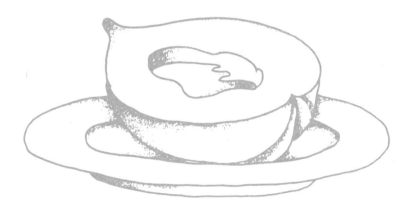

TWO EASY SALAD DRESSINGS*

Equipment you will need:
Small bowl or cup, 250 mL
Stirring spoon

Creamy Dressing*

Ingredients:

Mayonnaise or similar salad dressing	25 mL
Milk	25 mL
Honey	5 mL
Salt	1 mL

Mix all together in the cup and toss with the cabbage salad (page 53).

French-Type Dressing*

Ingredients:

Salad oil	45 mL
Catsup	15 mL
Sugar	5 mL
Salt	1 mL
Pinch of pepper	

Stir everything together in the cup and mix with the salad.

BLACK-EYED PEAS or BAKED BEANS**

Equipment you will need:
Saucepan, about 2 L
Casserole, about 2 L
Colander

Ingredients:

Black-eyed peas or navy beans	250 mL
Warm water	1 L
Salt	2 mL
Brown sugar	50 mL
Bacon	3 strips

Early in the morning or even the night before, wash the peas or beans and look them over carefully, discarding any that are bad. Cover with water and soak until they have swelled and all the wrinkles are out of them. This will take several hours.

Cook over low heat about three hours until the peas or beans are soft. Add more water if needed. When peas or beans are soft, drain into a colander in the sink and turn into the casserole. Mix in the salt and brown sugar and cover with three strips of bacon, each of which has been cut in half.

Bake at 175 degrees C (350 F) for one hour or until brown on top. Serves 4.

Eat with Swimmin' Chicken and milk gravy (page 44).

GREEK POTATOES*

Equipment you will need:
Shallow rectangular cake pan or baking dish
Paring knife
Long-handled spoon

Ingredients:

Potatoes, cut in quarters	4–5 medium
Butter or margarine	1 stick (about 125 mL)
Salt to taste	

Preheat the oven to 220 degrees C (about 425 F). Select a pan large enough so the potato quarters will lie flat. Peel and cut the potatoes. Melt the butter in the pan; this takes just a minute or two. Add the potatoes to the melted butter in the pan. Stir to coat the pieces all over with the melted butter. Bake in the oven 45 minutes or longer, until they are done and slightly browned. Using oven mitts, take the pan out of the oven and stir the potatoes once during the baking with a long-handled spoon. Before serving, season with salt.

Eat these special potatoes with a big salad, such as Vegetable Kingdom (page 57). They would also go well with open-faced Turtles (page 64). Remember your glass of milk and some fruit for dessert. Serves 4–5.

101 SALADS*

Equipment you will need:
Salad bowl large enough for your family
Cutting board
Paring knife
Large fork and spoon

Ingredients:	
Greens	1 L or more
Celery, cut up	125 mL
Radishes, sliced	3
Tomato, sliced or cut up	1
Onion, chopped	5 mL or more
Green pepper, slivered	¼
Ripe olives, quartered	4
Packaged croutons	50 mL

All salad makings should be cold. Plan on 250–500 mL of greens for each person, less for small children. Wash the greens carefully and dry on paper towels or in a spinner if you have one. Tear them into fork-sized pieces and measure into a salad bowl. Add all the other ingredients except the croutons. Just before serving, add the salad dressing, either your favorite prepared dressing or the French Type on page 54. Mix gently with a big fork and spoon until the dressing coats the pieces. Add the croutons and serve at once. Serves 4.

There are many different kinds of greens you might use. You might want to combine two kinds. Try endive or romaine, Boston or bibb lettuce, or leaf lettuce or spinach. You'll find other vegetables to use, too, such as carrots or kohlrabies or new peas. The ideas are endless.

Fruit salad may be made in the same way by substituting fruit for the vegetables. A little celery is good in fruit salad for its crunch (you can leave out the croutons). The Creamy Salad Dressing would be best on a fruit salad.

Sometimes refrigerated cooked vegetables added to greens will make a delicious next-day salad. Use your imagination and have fun. Be a salad person.

Hearty Vegetables

PEAS AND PEANUT SALAD*

Equipment you will need:
Salad bowl, about 1½ L
Stirring spoon

Ingredients:

Frozen peas	1 regular box (283 g)
Salted dry-roasted peanuts	100 mL
Mayonnaise or salad dressing	100 mL

Empty the frozen peas into the salad bowl and allow to thaw at room temperature for about half an hour. Mix the peanuts and the salad dressing with the uncooked thawed peas. Serve as a cold vegetable or on a lettuce leaf as a salad.

Isn't this a nutty way to get your vitamins? It's good, too.

Variations on this salad could be worked out by a creative cook. Chopped celery might be good mixed in, or a bit of pimento for color. Or try them both. Serves 4–6.

CLAM CHOWDER**

Equipment you will need:
Double boiler
Saucepan, 1 L or more
Stirring spoon or wire whisk
Pastry blender or chopper
Sharp knife
Cutting board

Ingredients:

Potato	1 medium
Water	150 mL
Butter or margarine	45 mL
Flour	45 mL
Milk	500 mL
Pimento, finely chopped	5 mL
Canned clams, minced	1 can, 225 g (about 8 oz.)
Salt	3 mL
Dash of cracked black pepper	
Onion, chopped	15 mL

Here is a soup that you might like to make your specialty. It is very good.

Peel the potato and cut into slices; then dice the slices. Bring to a boil in 150 mL water and simmer until just soft.

While the potatoes are cooking, melt the butter over low heat in the top of the double boiler and stir in the flour. Remember that you must put about 5 cm of water in the bottom of the double boiler. A wire whisk is good for mixing and helps get out the lumps. When the butter and flour are smooth, slowly add the milk while stirring. Cook until the mixture begins to thicken. Add pimento, minced clams and juice, salt and pepper.

When the potatoes are just soft, crush them a bit with the pastry blender, stir in the minced onion, and add to the soup mix. Continue cooking over hot water in the top of the double boiler. It takes at least half an hour of simmering the soup in the double boiler to bring out the flavor. If it seems a bit thick, add a little milk.

This is a hearty soup that is delicious served with crackers and a green salad (page 55), or perhaps some of the Vegetable Kingdom (page 57) already in the refrigerator. Serves 4. Don't forget some fruit for dessert.

THE VEGETABLE KINGDOM**

Equipment you will need:
Medium-sized saucepan
Sharp knife
Cutting board
Large bowl
Covered containers for storing in refrigerator

Ingredients:

Frozen mixed vegetables	2 boxes (about 285 g each)
Red kidney beans, drained	1 can (about 680 g)
Celery, chopped fine	8 stalks
Green pepper, chopped fine	1
Onion, chopped fine	1 small

Dressing

Ingredients:

Flour	30 mL
Sugar or honey	375 mL
Vinegar	250 mL
Prepared mustard	60 mL

You can forget the "I hate vegetables" song. This is a crunchy combination of vegetables in a delicious sauce that will make a vegetable lover out of everybody. Serve it as a salad on lettuce or as a relish, or just keep it cold in the refrigerator for after-school munching.

Cook the two packages of mixed vegetables in salted water until just done. They should still be crisp. Drain and cool. Vegetables can be cooled more quickly by emptying them into a sieve or colander and mixing with ice cubes. While the vegetables are cooling, make the sauce.

Mix the flour and sugar together and add the vinegar, stirring. Cook until the mixture thickens. Remove from range. Measure the mustard into a cup; add a little of the sugar-vinegar mixture and blend well; then add it all to the sugar-vinegar mixture and stir in well. Chill or at least cool it completely.

While the sauce and vegetables are cooling, chop the celery, green pepper, and onion. Add to the cooled mixed vegetables and kidney beans. Pour the cooled sauce over. Mix and store in the refrigerator until ready to use.

This recipe makes 3 liters. It keeps well for several days in the refrigerator if tightly covered. If it seems too strong when you take it out of the refrigerator, drain some of the sauce.

THREE HOT SANDWICHES**

Equipment you will need:
Spreading knife
Mixing bowl
Cookie sheet
Aluminum foil

Hot Ham and Cheese Bunwitches

Ingredients:

Hamburger buns	8
Butter, mustard, and mayonnaise	
Ham	8 slices
Swiss or Muenster cheese	8 slices

Spread buns with butter, mustard, and mayonnaise. Cover with ham and cheese. Wrap in aluminum foil. Bake 15 minutes at 175 degrees C (350 F). Serves 8.

Turtles, or Slumber Party Burgers

Ingredients:

Hamburger buns	4
Ground beef	500 mL (560 g, about 1¼ lbs.)
Sweet pickle relish	75 mL
Salt	5 mL
Pepper to taste	
Mustard	30 mL
Catsup	45 mL
Onion, chopped	1 small

Split hamburger buns in half. Mix meat with other ingredients in a bowl and spread on bun halves. Be sure to spread the mixture to the edges of each bun so they won't burn. Place under preheated broiler at 160 degrees C (325 F) for 10 minutes. Watch carefully so the buns don't burn. Makes 8 open-faced sandwiches.

Hot Tuna Sandwiches

Ingredients:

Canned tuna	1 can, 187 g (about 6½ oz.)
Celery, cut fine	1 stalk
Mayonnaise or salad dressing	50 mL
Bean sprouts (optional)	50 mL
Natural wheat bread or buns	4 slices, toasted
Cheddar or processed cheese	½ slice for each bread slice

Drain the tuna, add chopped celery, salad dressing, and bean sprouts. Spread on slices of toast or toasted buns. Top with a slice of cheese. Heat broiler to 150 degrees C (300 F) and broil slowly until the cheese bubbles. Watch carefully. Be sure you have spread the mixture to the edges or they may burn before the sandwiches are cooked. Serves 4.

SHIMMY SALAD**

Equipment you will need:
Fancy salad mold, about 2 L
Saucepan, about 2 L
Stirring spoon
Paring knife

Ingredients:

Apple juice	500 mL
Lime-flavored gelatin	1 large box (about 200 g)
Salt	1 mL
Lemon juice	45 mL
Ginger ale	1 bottle, 350 mL (about 12 oz.)
Banana, peeled, sliced	1
Pineapple chunks, drained, *or* mandarin orange sections	1 can, about 235 mL (12 oz.)
Apples, red ones	2

Measure the apple juice and put in the saucepan along with the flavored gelatin. Stir over low heat until the gelatin is completely dissolved. Remove from heat. Add the salt and lemon juice and cool. Add the ginger ale. When the mixture is cool, pour about one-third in the bottom of the salad mold. Chill by placing the mold in a large dish with ice water. Chill the remainder in the saucepan.

Meanwhile, cut the banana and mix with the drained pineapple or orange sections. Wash the apples but don't peel them. Cut in quarters and remove the cores. Dice one apple and add it to the fruit mixture, but save the other to cut into slices.

When the gelatin mixture in the bottom of the mold is set, stand the apple sections in it with the skin side to the bottom of the mold. Mix the rest of the fruit with the remaining gelatin and carefully spoon it into the mold. Take care not to tip over any of the apple sections. Chill at least 2 hours in the refrigerator.

When ready to serve, unmold the salad. You may need some help with this. Fill the sink or a large pan with warm water. Carefully loosen the salad around the edge with a knife. Hold the mold in the warm water for about a minute. Flip quickly onto a plate and arrange lettuce leaves around it.

If you flip it fast enough, you will have a lovely shimmering salad that serves 8–10 people. Beautiful!

HAMBURGER SOUP**

Equipment you will need:
Large heavy saucepan
Frying pan
Plastic spatula or slotted spoon
Sharp knife
Cutting board

Ingredients:

Ground beef	500 mL (560 g, about 1¼ lbs.)
Salad oil	15 mL
Butter or margarine	45 mL
Celery, sliced	125 mL
Carrots, sliced	125 mL
Onion, chopped	50 mL
Potatoes, peeled and cubed	180 mL
Water	1 L
Tomatoes, fresh or canned, chopped	180 mL
Salt and pepper to taste	

Brown the ground beef in a frying pan with salad oil. Turn off the heat. Melt the butter in a deep saucepan and stir-fry all the vegetables except the tomatoes until lightly browned. Turn the heat to low. Lift the browned meat out of the frying pan, using the spatula or a slotted spoon, and add it to the vegetables. Add the water. Add tomatoes, and salt and pepper to taste. Simmer on low heat about 30 minutes. Serve hot with saltine crackers. Serves about 6.

HOT OR COLD POTATO SALAD**

Equipment you will need:
Large saucepan
Medium-sized mixing bowl, 1 or 2 L
Cutting board
Sharp knife

Ingredients:

Potatoes	5 medium or 9 small ones
Hard-boiled eggs	3
Celery, chopped	250 mL
Mayonnaise	125 mL
Sweet pickle juice	60 mL
Onion, chopped	25 mL
Fresh parsley, chopped	60 mL
Salt and pepper to taste	
Radishes, sliced thin	2
Paprika	

This potato salad is just as good served warm in the winter as it is served cold in the summer. If you plan to serve it warm, you probably would not garnish it with the sliced radishes.

Boil the potatoes with the skins on until just fork tender. Remember to turn down the heat when they start boiling so they just simmer until they are done but are still firm. This may take close to 30 minutes. You can boil the eggs at the same time (see page 29 for instructions). Drain the potatoes and allow to cool until you can handle them. Cool the eggs separately under running water. When cool enough, peel off the shells.

Meantime, chop the celery. Mix the mayonnaise and pickle juice in the bowl and add the onion. When the potatoes are cool enough to handle, peel them and dice them into the bowl. Toss lightly.

If serving warm, add the chopped celery and parsley and mix. Taste and season with salt and pepper. Serve at once, garnished with sliced hard-boiled eggs. If serving cold, add the celery, parsley, salt, and pepper, and chill in the refrigerator. Serve decorated with the radish slices and the eggs, halved and sprinkled with paprika. Serves 4–5.

STONE SOUP*

Equipment you will need:
Saucepan, about 2 L
Sharp knife
Cutting board

Ingredients:

Leftover chicken	125 mL (or more)
Bouillon cube	1
Water	500 mL
Celery and celery tops, washed	
and chopped fine	25 mL
Onion, chopped	2 mL
Uncooked noodles	125 mL
Salt to taste	

Cut the meat from the chicken and dice it. Heat the bouillon cube with the chicken in the water, add celery tops, celery, onion, and noodles. Simmer for about 30 minutes. Taste and add salt if needed. Serves 2.

If you add half a tomato, cut up, and a carrot, your soup will be even better. Use your imagination when making soup. This is a thrifty way to use leftovers. A cheese sandwich and a glass of milk make a good lunch with Stone Soup.

If you want to try beef soup, ask your mother to buy or save a nice big bone from a roast. If there is a little meat on it, that would be good. Cover it with cold water and bring it to a boil. Turn the heat low and then use your imagination about adding vegetables. Try adding a few at a time. If you add potatoes, it will make a thicker soup. Cut everything fine. Watch your soup closely and taste it from time to time to see how the flavor is developing. Always be sure to cool the sample before you taste it. Really good cooks make soup this way.

You could make soup with a ham bone, too. Combine it with split peas or black-eyed peas for a really great soup. This kind needs all-day cooking and plenty of watching. Be sure to stir it often. At the end you may want to thin your ham and pea soup with a little warm milk.

Invent your own favorite soup. Experiment a bit and become famous in your family for your special soup.

REMEMBER: Before you start any recipe, read the "Before You Begin" section on pp. 11–12 and the safety rules on pp. 13–14.

THE BEST CHICKEN SALAD YOU EVER ATE***

Equipment you will need:
Large mixing bowl
Cutting board
Paring knife
2 saucepans, one large for chicken breasts,
   one medium-sized for eggs
Small frying pan

Ingredients:

Hard-boiled eggs, chopped	2
Chicken breasts, cooked, and diced (about 6)	750 mL
Lemon juice	45 mL
Salt	5 mL
Celery, chopped	250 mL
Seedless green grapes, halved	250 mL
Mayonnaise	165 mL
Toasted almonds, slivered	100 mL

This salad is best made the night before and chilled overnight in the refrigerator. It isn't easy to make and takes a little time, but it's worth the trouble.

Simmer the eggs in hot water for 15–20 minutes. (See page 29 on hard-boiling eggs.) Meanwhile, simmer the chicken breasts in enough water to cover them for about 40 minutes or until tender. Cool. Reserve the broth to use as soup. Cut and dice the chicken and sprinkle with lemon juice and salt. Let stand overnight in the refrigerator or at least for several hours. When the chicken has been sufficiently chilled, add the remaining ingredients (except the toasted almonds) and toss lightly. Sprinkle with toasted almonds (see directions below). Serve on lettuce. Serves 8.

How to toast the almonds: Melt 15 mL butter or margarine over low heat in a small frying pan. Add the slivered nuts and watch carefully. Stir often so they brown evenly. When just browned but not burned, drain and cool the nuts on a piece of paper toweling.

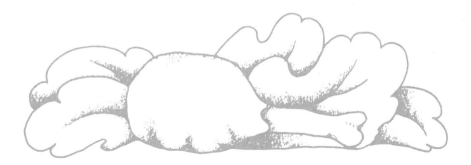

Soup Pot
and
Sandwich
Spread